Revolutionary
Change

BASIC STUDIES IN POLITICS

Under the Editorship of

SHELDON S. WOLIN

University of California, Berkeley

CHALMERS JOHNSON

Department of Political Science
University of California, Berkeley

Revolutionary
Change

LITTLE, BROWN AND COMPANY
Boston

LIBRARY OF CONGRESS CATALOG CARD NO. 66-26489

SECOND PRINTING

Published simultaneously in Canada
by Little, Brown & Company (Canada) Limited

PRINTED IN THE UNITED STATES OF AMERICA

Foreword

LIKE SO MANY areas of human knowledge to-
day, the study of politics and political institutions is undergoing
significant changes. A quarter-century ago only a few voices
challenged the prevailing consensus regarding the methods of
political science, the choice of problems, and the relative weight
assigned to the "factors" shaping political events, actions, and behavior. Since then a revolution of uncertain proportions has occurred, one that has been variously described as "the behavioral
movement" or "social science." It has visibly altered the climate
of political science and it has deeply affected the outlook of the
political scientist. No longer does he believe that political science
is a self-contained field. It has become second nature for him to
utilize methods, concepts, and data drawn from a wide range of
academic disciplines, such as sociology, psychology, and economics.

A marked self-consciousness about methods of inquiry characterizes much of the contemporary literature, whereas thirty years
ago only a few political scientists were troubled by this concern.
Today's political scientist is receptive to quantitative techniques,
eager to emphasize measurement, prepared to devise complex clas-

sifications of empirical data, ready to experiment with abstract models, and engrossed with the intricacies of preparing questionnaires and organizing surveys of public opinion. These changes in method have also affected the outlook and the language of political science. Where his predecessors talked of "comparative government," he is apt to talk of "comparative political systems"; where they referred to "the process of government," he prefers to examine "the theory of decision-making"; and where they spoke simply of "political theory," he will, more often than not, insist on a distinction between "normative theory" and "empirical theory," and depending on his candor or concerns, will assert that his main interest lies with the latter. It is perhaps inevitable that a moderate reaction should set in and that questions should be raised among political scientists about whether they have not gone too far and too fast. There is an uneasiness that some settled issues ought to be reopened; that important features of politics have been ignored; that questions of choice and value have to be restored to a central position; and that the wonder of politics has been lost amidst the preoccupation with abstractions, graphs, and mathematical tables.

In the light of these changes and uncertainties there is good reason for political scientists and political theorists to reflect on the changing nature of their field of study and to report to a less specialized, but no less interested, audience how political events, practices, and behavior appear to the contemporary political scientist; what way or ways of looking at these matters he has found most useful and fruitful; and what problems he considers to be genuine and important.

This series of books was designed for such a purpose. The authors do not attempt to provide simply a digest of relevant facts, but to offer reflections and systematic analyses of the more significant and interesting areas of political science and political theory. Some concentrate upon familiar topics, such as federalism and political parties, but they seek to suggest the theoretically interesting problems raised by these traditional themes. Other studies, such as those dealing with political theory and ideology, proceed on a more theoretical plane, but with the explicit intention of indicating their relevance to the empirical concerns of political science. The standard set for this volume by Professor Johnson and for all the others is, I hope, within the best tradition of political science: the standard of reflective inquiry and informed analysis.

Sometimes a political problem captures the attention of theorists because of its novelty, other times because of its magnitude or scale. The phenomenon of revolution manages to combine both novelty and magnitude. Although history provides many instances of coups, revolts, and mass uprisings, there are strong reasons for believing that modern revolutions display so many striking differences that they cannot be treated as belonging to the same species. Burke's powerful polemic against the French Revolution had been based on just such a belief; he characterized its distinguishing feature as "a revolution of doctrine and theoretic dogma," what we would call an ideological revolution. Other writers have remarked upon the organized, premeditated quality of revolutions, particularly those of the nineteenth and twentieth centuries. The professional revolutionary is the unique creation of modern times and so is the "underground culture" which usually sustains him.

Yet, in the last analysis, there are two features of modern revolutions which stand out. One is the scale of upheaval; whole societies have been overturned and redirected. The most spectacular examples would be the French Revolution of 1789, the Bolshevik Revolution, and the recent Chinese Revolution. The second feature is the tendency of these revolutions to extend themselves in time and space. The French Revolution was carried to many parts of Europe; and France itself experienced recurring revolutionary crises throughout the nineteenth century. In our own time the radiating effects of Russian and Chinese Communism have posed major problems for Western and non-Western statesmen. One is tempted to say of revolution what Tocqueville said of equality: it is universal, lasting, seemingly beyond human control, and all events as well as all men contribute to its increase.

Despite the novel aspects of modern revolutions, the great political writers of the past have been enormously influential in defining the problems and furnishing concepts for analyzing revolutionary phenomena. Thucydides, Plato, and Aristotle established

the fundamental contraries of "order" and revolution; they drew
attention to the connections between class conflict and political
change and to the relationships between conflicting economic
interests and conflicting political values; and they took account of
the distinction between the broad underlying causes of instability
and the immediate "occasion" that triggered upheaval. Later
writers, such as Polybius, called attention to the way in which
one revolutionary change in regime prepared the way for another; this theory of political "cycles" opened the possibility that
these successive changes could be predicted in advance. The great
English revolution of the seventeenth century inspired Harring-
ton's famous thesis that revolution was produced when the
distribution of political authority was incongruent with the distribution of economic power within a society. In the next century
Burke discovered the significance of ideology and the peculiar
blend of rationalism and passion that supplied an important dynamic to revolution. The nineteenth century produced the two
greatest theorists of revolution, Alexis de Tocqueville and Karl
Marx: the one a master analyst of political and social causes, the
other of economic causes. Tocqueville taught his readers to seek
the imperceptible beginnings of 1789 in the distant past, in the
gradual development of the centralized bureaucracy which gradually stifled *l'ancien régime* and destroyed the aristocracy as a
political class. In Marx, revolution found its tragedian who concluded his epical account of historical transformations with the
pronouncement that revolution was man's fate as well as his hope;
revolution, he declared, was inherent in the developing structure
of all modern societies.

For all of its scientific trappings, Marxian theory retained that
traditional element of wonder and amazement at the sheer spec-
tacle of revolution. The heroic and epic style which theorists have
tended to assume in the presence of revolution has reflected their
determination to do justice to the extraordinary quality of revolutions. Revolution has meant drastic transformation in the lives,
relationships, and values of the members of society; the elimination of old institutions and the creation of new ones; the displacement of one group from power and the succession of
another. Above all, revolution has meant the widespread use of

violence and the organization of destruction. The epic style has the effect of making actors and events appear larger than life; revolutions have seemed almost preternatural occurrences.

The contemporary social scientist is ready to acknowledge his intellectual debts to these older theories of revolution, but he is dissatisfied with their explanatory value. Convinced that the study of revolution cannot attain scientific or truly empirical status as long as revolutions are analyzed in terms of their uniqueness, or explained by long-run historical "forces," or attributed to giant actors, the social scientist attempts to locate revolutions in a broader class of social phenomena which he believes is susceptible to empirical explanation.

In the present study Professor Johnson has assimilated revolution under the more comprehensive category of "social change" and thereby availed himself of the extensive social scientific research on that subject. Further, instead of analyzing revolutions as unique or as products of local conditions, he has looked upon them as situations possible within any social system. The concept of a social system, which is carefully elaborated in Chapter Three, enables him to discuss revolutions in a comparative way and to point towards the possibility of establishing comprehensive empirical generalizations. This study is particularly noteworthy for its breadth and range of evidence. He has joined theories and analyses of Western societies to his own specialized acquaintance with Far Eastern societies. The result is a stimulating and tightly-reasoned contribution to our understanding of a fundamental problem.

Sheldon S. Wolin

UNIVERSITY OF CALIFORNIA, BERKELEY

Preface

THIS BOOK was originally conceived as an introduction to the theoretical problems encountered in trying to conceptualize revolution. In preparing my first formulation of these
problems and in continuing to grapple with the inadequacies of
that attempt, I came to the conclusion that revolution is inseparable from the social context in which it occurs.*

Revolution is not a discrete, relatively isolable, purely political
phenomenon; the factors that contribute to it are as manifold as
the elements comprising society itself, and abstract generalizations
about revolution must reflect this extreme complexity. The analyst
must therefore make use of sociological, psychological, military,
and economic, as well as political, concepts and data. Because I
have had to be as much concerned in this study with the analysis
of society as with the analysis of revolution, and because I have
borrowed extensively from the theoretical literature of scholarly

---

* Compare this volume with my *Revolution and the Social System* (Stanford, Calif.: Hoover Institution Studies, No. 3, 1964), originally presented
to the panel on "Theories of Modern Revolution and Violence," American
Political Science Association Annual Meeting, 1963, under the chairmanship
of Professor Sheldon S. Wolin.

fields other than my own, I hope that my interpretations do not pain too greatly the sociologists, anthropologists, philosophers, and social psychologists to whom I am indebted. By way of justifying my presumption, I am convinced that these specialists too must become borrowers if they intend to analyze revolution in its full complexity.

The analytical study of revolution is not in its infancy, but much of the earlier work on revolution reveals the restricted disciplinary perspectives held by the various writers. As a consequence, this intellectual heritage offers only piecemeal insights into the phenomenon of revolution. Economists, either inspired by or arguing with Marx, seem always to conclude that economic trends lie at the base of revolutionary movements. Social psychologists, using their specialized tools for conceptualizing personality formation, have explored the dimensions of the rebellious personality. Historians have studied the complex decisions of and relationships among the parties to a revolutionary struggle, and they have attempted to compare revolutions on the basis of these studies. And political philosophers have explored the adequacy of various expressions of value in engendering or dissipating the consent of the governed in particular types of regimes. It is crucial to realize that all these, and several other, perspectives must be incorporated into any comprehensive model of revolutionary process.

In my opinion, the way to achieve this synthesis is not through a so-called "interdisciplinary colloquium." What is required is a conceptual paradigm of the functional society — one that reveals the interrelationships between value, economic necessity, acceptable personality configurations, social control, and historical actions. Within such a paradigm we can then begin to isolate the multivariant pressures, structural characteristics, and events that combine to produce the *revolutionary* social system.

The model of the social system presented in this book — a synthesis of the so-called "coercion" and "value" theories of society — is offered on its merits, not simply as a "heuristic device." A good deal of controversy surrounds one of its central propositions — namely, the portrayal of society in a state of homeostatic equilibrium. As a scholar trained in the political history of Far Eastern societies, I do not find this model to be at variance with my empirical data. In fact, my own intellectual experience leads me to the conclusion that change in social structure, revolutionary or otherwise, is not a continuous process. Structural change occurs more frequently in fits and starts, in response to concrete, identifiable political and social disturbances of societal equilibrium. Because I have found this model to be efficient in understanding the most long-lived social systems on earth, I believe that its generalized use can be recommended on more substantial grounds than merely as a benchmark from which to begin our search for a more genuine social "reality." In any case, I am convinced that intellectual discourse over this problem can be effective only in the context of paradigm-testing, through comparative and case studies, which in turn may lead to the development of a more powerful paradigmatic model of the social system. In the absence of an informing paradigm that unites the elements of social action, writing on the subject of revolution has come closer to the genres of literature and belles lettres than to social science.*

This book was written at the University of California, Berkeley, during the years 1963 to 1965. In the autumn of 1964, the University was rocked by a student rebellion that it was my good fortune to observe and to learn from. In reflecting on the causes of the students' resort to violence against the University, I believe that the conceptual framework developed in this volume can be used to interpret the events there. In terms of the larger, remote causes, the University was beset by problems of overcrowding, changing curriculum, incoherent priorities, and very rapid expansion — problems that reflected many of the basic changes going on in the society which it serves. But these conditions did not cause the rebellion; they created the demands for change within the University. The second set of remote causes was the students' loss of confidence in the ability, and the authority, of the governors of the University to bring the institution's values and environment into congruence. By governors, I include the faculty along with the full-time administrators; dissension within the

---

* For a complete elaboration of how paradigms function in scientific research, see Thomas Kuhn, *The Structure of Scientific Revolutions* (Chicago: University of Chicago Press, 1962).

"elite" promoted this revolution in the same way that Plato predicted it would in the Eighth Book of the *Republic*. The stage having been set, the actual outbreak of violence was accelerated by an incident, as in so many other cases of revolutionary behavior.

In addition to the systemic causes of the revolt, this particular instance manifested most other characteristics of revolution. An ideological "goal culture" influenced the leaders of the revolt, individuals joined the movement for the most heterodox motives, a superbly appropriate strategy of revolution was pursued by the leadership, and the overt violence was ultimately suppressed by the use of overwhelming force. The Berkeley revolution was not a pretty sight — it was immensely damaging to the values of the particular social system, as all revolutions are — but it did cause processual change to be inaugurated.* I retain the conviction, however, that revolution is always avoidable if only the creative potentialities of political organization can be realized. Revolution is an acceptable means of change only when purposive policies of change are not forthcoming. As Rousseau has written, "The nature of things does not madden us: only ill-will does."

More important than being a locale of revolution, Berkeley has influenced me, and this book, through my education there as a student and through the stimulation I continue to receive from my colleagues and students in the Department of Political Science. The ideas presented in this book were first elaborated and explored in the Political Science Department's graduate seminar on revolutionary change, now in its fifth year, and I would like to acknowledge the contribution made by the students of that seminar.

Mr. Robert Smith, a graduate student in political science, assisted me in gathering statistics for Chapter Six, and I received a grant from the Rockefeller Foundation research funds, administered by the Department of Political Science, in order to carry on this research. The book was completed in Hong Kong where, supported by the Social Science Research Council, I returned

---

* For further information on the Berkeley revolution, see Seymour M. Lipset and Sheldon S. Wolin, eds., *The Berkeley Student Revolt, Facts and Interpretations* (New York: Doubleday Anchor Books, 1965).

from my excursion into social theory to the study of the greatest revolution of our time — that which occurred in China.

Sheila K. Johnson, my wife, edited and typed the entire manuscript, and she greatly facilitated my introduction to the theoretical literature of social anthropology. Needless to say, I retain responsibility for all interpretations and conclusions reached in this study.

Chalmers Johnson

UNIVERSITY OF CALIFORNIA, BERKELEY

Table
of contents

xvii

Woe to him that claims obedience when it is not due;
Woe to him that refuses it when it is.

THOMAS CARLYLE

Revolutionary
Change

I

Revolution:
the implications
of a political concept

SIXTY YEARS AGO Arthur Bauer of the University
of Paris began his book on revolution with a definition that has
withstood the tests of one of the most revolutionary half-centuries
in history. "Les révolutions," he wrote, "sont les changements
tentés ou réalisés par la force dans la constitution des sociétés."[1]
All of the elements of the elusive concept of revolution are here.
Revolutions are social changes. Sometimes they succeed; often
they fail. Revolutionary change is a special kind of social change,
one that involves the intrusion of violence into civil social relations. And revolution, both as a form of behavior and as a concept,
concerns the most basic level of man's communal existence — its
constitution, in the Aristotelian sense of the principles of distributive justice prevailing in a particular society.

If a definition were all that is required to permit us to recognize
and understand revolutions when they occur, Bauer has provided
us with one. But before we can begin to appreciate the implications of Bauer's definition, we must recognize that the elements of

his, or any other, definition of revolution are themselves in need
of explanation and definition. What is social change, of which
revolution is one particular configuration? Why do revolutions
sometimes succeed, and what do we mean by success in this context? What is violence, of which insurrection — the certain mark
of either rebellion or revolution — is also only one particular configuration? And what is it about formally constituted regimes that
breeds internal demands for periodic renovation? The study of
revolution is the attempt to ask these questions with rigor and
penetration. This essay, in turn, is an attempt to continue a dia-
logue over these questions that is as old as man's social self-aware-
ness.

It has sometimes been supposed that political theory has very
little to say on the subject of either violence or revolution. Both
are seen as signs of the failure of politics and hence considered outside the range of interests of the political theorist.[2] In terms of the
history of Western political philosophy it is occasionally argued,
for example, that Edmund Burke was the first theorist of revolution and that all serious theoretical writing on revolutions can be
dated from the French Revolution and its political reverberations.
On a purely historical level there is some evidence for this view.
The modern age, characterized by revolutionary threats to the
nation-state, did begin in 1789. Analytically speaking, however,
the idea of revolution was implicit in the first organized society.

The English word "revolution" is particularly inadequate in
conveying the meaning of purposive political violence. In its political sense, "revolution" did not begin to be used until the late
Renaissance, but much older meanings (e.g., the "revolutions" of
the planets) give the word overtones that suggest there are forces
in human affairs comparable to the superhuman forces governing
the universe.[3] We can come considerably closer to one of the
political implications of revolution by looking at it in the oldest
continuously extant language on earth — Chinese. In Chinese "revolution" is the complement to another word referring to the right
to rule — the authority — of the Chinese Emperor. *T'ien-ming*
天命 means literally "the mandate of heaven," whereas *ke-ming*
革命 which we translate as revolution, means "to withdraw the

mandate." The idea of revolution in Chinese is thus unintelligible without a prior knowledge of the mandate of heaven, the Confucian doctrine wherein the Emperor is alleged to possess superior virtue and is thereby authorized to rule.

Although the English word implies no such thing, the Western concept of revolution is similarly tied to a vision of political organization in which revolt is unnecessary and therefore unjustifiable. This is the first point to be made about the study of revolutions in general or of any one in particular: revolutions must be studied in the context of the social systems in which they occur. The analysis of revolution intermeshes with the analysis of viable, functioning societies, and any attempt to separate the two concepts impairs the usefulness of both. Some scholars who have failed to take the contingent nature of revolution seriously have explored revolutionary behavior as if it were a relatively isolable and discrete phenomenon. They have, in effect, reduced the sociology of revolution to the comparative study of the techniques for seizing power. Unfortunately for them there is a great deal more to the problem of revolution than the forms which insurrection may take, and such questions as whether revolutionaries should or should not poison a city's water supply are among the least interesting aspects of the resort to revolution in a society.

The study of society and revolution is somewhat analogous to the study of physiology and pathology: a knowledge of morbid conditions in animals depends upon a knowledge of healthy conditions in the same species. The analogy, however, is not exact. Whereas physiology and pathology are analytically distinct investigations, corresponding to different states of an organism, the sociology of functional societies comes logically before the sociology of revolution. This is true because social organization itself is intended to restrict or minimize violence among the people united in a society, both purposefully in terms of the conscious policies pursued by a society's members and functionally in terms of one of the unintended consequences of the value-coordinated division of labor. Therefore in order to perceive why a revolution, signifying the return to a form of violence, occurs, we must have a knowledge of how and why the social barriers against violence have collapsed or have been breached.

Aristotle was the first political theorist to show that revolutions are contextually specific — that is, that the key to understanding why men want to change their social relations is to grasp how men think that their society ought to be organized. Aristotle summarized his opinion on this subject by offering some examples: "The universal and chief cause of . . . revolutionary feeling [is] . . . the desire of equality, when men think that they are equal to others who have more than themselves; or, again, the desire of inequality and superiority, when conceiving themselves to be superior they think that they have not more but the same or less than their inferiors; pretensions which may and may not be just."[4] Although Aristotle uses the term "revolutionary feeling" in a much broader sense than we do — he is concerned with the more inclusive phenomenon of political instability and social change, of which violent revolution is only one important manifestation — he emphasizes that revolution must be derived from the study of an affirmative social order with which men have become dissatisfied. Aristotle argues that revolutionary feelings do not exist when men's conceptions of themselves are faithfully mirrored in the principles upon which their society is organized.

Speaking in more general terms, we may say that the concept of revolution occupies a niche in a hierarchy of broader and more abstract concepts concerned with the organization of men's social interdependence. In order to reach this analytical niche we must begin by asking the broadest kind of questions: How is order and stability possible in human relations? What are the principles that men adopt in order to stabilize and legitimatize the cooperation forced upon them by their economic and political geography? In what manner do societies exist and persist? If we are able to achieve some intellectual agreement on these questions, we may then descend to the next analytical level and ask what causes stable societies to become unstable and to change. In making this progression from one category of political questions to another, we are not moving from one subject matter to another (as, for example, from physiology to pathology). The study of social change is in a sense identical with the study of the determinants of social order. As the quote from Aristotle implies, any affirmation of a basis for order is potentially discriminatory when seen from a different point of view, and therein lies one important source of the seeds of instability. To study social change is simply to focus more carefully upon the already familiar terrain of social integration; it is not a matter of shifting to an entirely different locale.

Even when concentrating upon the strains in a viable society that may give rise to demands for change, we are a long way from isolating the phenomenon of revolution. Revolution is not the same thing as social change; it is a form of social change. Of equal, or greater, importance in understanding why violent revolutions sometimes occur is an appreciation of how the members of certain societies have been able to make basic changes *without* resorting to violence. The radical changes that occurred in the United States during the New Deal, or the process whereby Japan changed from a feudal to a modern state, or the modifications that English government underwent in response to industrialization, were all accomplished without resort to revolution.

Sometimes we speak of changes such as these as "revolutionary," using the already metaphorical word "revolution" in a still more metaphorical sense to mean changes of great magnitude (e.g., the "industrial revolution"). But the concept of revolution in political analysis refers specifically to the form of change that occurred, for example, in France in 1789, in Russia in 1917, and in China in 1949. One reason why revolutions took place in these societies is that non-revolutionary change had already failed — a point that should demonstrate the need to study the more general phenomenon of social change before we can turn to revolution itself. Not only must we study social change, we must try to isolate the determinants of non-revolutionary change so that we can better understand the determinants of the revolutionary situation. Aristotle has suggested that the seeds of instability and change are to be found in the form of the social structure itself, but we shall find that structurally-generated dissatisfactions are only one possible source of either change or revolution.

To argue that revolutions must be studied within the context of the social systems in which they occur is not to deny the value of comparative analyses of revolutions. The anthropologist A. R. Radcliffe-Brown once argued that comparison is the form that experimentation takes in the social sciences, and much of the research done on revolutions has utilized the technique of comparing revolutions. Gaetano Salvemini, for example, writing on the nature of history and of the social sciences, advocates that "To determine whether revolutions are governed by constant laws, there is only one method: we must compare one with the other the greatest possible number of revolutions, . . . and we must see whether between these phenomena so far apart in time and space there can be discovered similarities or dissimilarities which are constant."[5] Crane Brinton, in his justly famous book, *Anatomy of Revolution*, attempted to do just that by comparing the English, American, French, and Russian revolutions.[6]

However, before the comparative method can be used effectively, there must be some agreement on what is being compared and on the variables that are to be used as a basis for discovering differences and similarities. Precisely because there is so little agreement on how to conceptualize revolution, and because revolution has often been treated in isolation from other political phenomena, comparative analyses of revolutions have commonly been a source of further confusion. In 1964, Harry Eckstein, summarizing the conclusions of a symposium on the sociology of revolution, argued that "The most urgent pre-theoretical need in internal war [i.e., revolution] studies today is the development, even if only tentative, of basic descriptive categories in terms of which the basic features of internal wars can be identified, in terms of which their nuances and broader features can be depicted in general structural concepts, classes (or types) constructed, and resemblances of cases to one another or to types accurately assessed."[7]

By disregarding the social system (and its condition) within which a revolution occurs, some scholars have lost track of the very idea they sought to analyze. "To withdraw the mandate" does not make much sense without the prior existence of a "mandate." Peasant jacqueries, urban insurrections, military coups d'état, conspiracies plotted by revolutionary associations, and domestically-supported counterrevolutions are all examples of rebellion or revolution; and all are marked by the acceptance of violence by certain members of the society in order to cause the society to change. However, to compare these events merely in terms of

their forms or participants is to ignore the deeper political significance of these forms or of the fact that certain social groups, and
not others, resorted to revolution.

The comparative method, when applied to revolutions, must be
devoted to comparing potentially revolutionary societies. In order
to focus on potentially revolutionary societies, major attention
must be given to societies that appear to be immune to revolution
and to the circumstances wherein some of these societies lose their
immunity. The problem of conceptualizing revolutions is closely
analogous to the problem of conceptualizing mental illness. The
latter problem was solved only when scholars agreed that "mental
illness can be understood — and *only* understood — in its biographical setting. [It] makes sense only in terms of the patient's attempt
at solving a problem in his living and to think of it as a mere disorder in some mechanism is fruitless." [8]

Another way of stressing the contingent nature of the concept
of revolution is to examine it as a form of violence. Despite all
evidence to the contrary, some scholars of revolution persist in
refusing to accept the idea that an irreducible element of any revolution is the resort to, or acceptance of, violence. Even many revolutionaries take pains to develop strategies of revolution which
they can characterize as "nonviolent." As we shall see, "nonviolent
revolution," so long as these words retain any precise meaning
whatsoever, is a contradiction in terms. "Nonviolent revolution"
is actually the name of a revolutionary strategy containing a
built-in propaganda appeal to persons holding certain definable
values. Nevertheless, it is quite true that many revolutions have
been accomplished without any blood flowing in the gutters or a
single death being caused. What then, sociologically speaking, do
we mean by violence? This question is also basic to the analysis of
revolution.

One of the simplest things that can be said about revolutions is
that they are forms of human behavior — that is, they are not
something analogous to earthquakes or sunspots. As a form of human behavior, revolution is a proper object for social science
research in the broad sense in which we understand all social
sciences to be "behavioral sciences." Following Max Weber, we
may classify human behavior into two broad types: "action" and

"social action." According to Weber, action is "all human behavior when and in so far as the acting individual attaches a subjective meaning to it." In this sense bodily or mental processes of which we are not aware are not "action," although our responses to the symptoms of these processes may be. One particular form of action is "social action." Again according to Weber, "action is social in so far as by virtue of the subjective meaning attached to it by the acting individual (or individuals), it takes account of the behavior of others and is thereby oriented in its course."[9]

If we carry Weber's idea of orientation to others a stage further and specify that orientation occurs because the acting individual possesses stable *expectations* of the behavior and responses to behavior of identifiable individuals in a full range of culturally-circumscribed social situations, then we have a rough, introductory approximation of the idea of social action *in a social system*. Virtually every major theorist of society holds that the *sine qua non* of a society (both conceptually and concretely) is the possession of mutual expectations by members of the society, allowing them to orient their behavior to each other. The very concept of the division of labor depends upon such mutual expectations, and man's ability to orient his behavior to that of others is a prerequisite for the complex human interaction that characterizes even the most rudimentary society.

Given this formal analysis of social action in a social system, we may define violence as action that deliberately or unintentionally disorients the behavior of others. Violence is either behavior which is impossible for others to orient themselves to or behavior which is deliberately intended to prevent orientation and the development of stable expectations with regard to it. Violence is not necessarily brutality, or insensitivity, or the antithesis of empathy; as we shall see in a later chapter, the capacity of human beings to adjust and orient themselves to these forms of behavior is almost limitless, as for example in the concentration camps of World War II. Violence is "antisocial action," and in a political context violence, like revolution, is a contingent concept dependent upon the prior existence of a system of social action within which it takes place. Despite the fact that wars reveal many instances of systematic orientation among the belligerents, the radical ideal of war and of waging it successfully constitutes the quintessence of violence.

War among men and social interaction among men are antipodal concepts, as the greatest theorist of violence, Thomas Hobbes, sought to show in his *Leviathan*. However, the relationship between war and society is not simply that of conceptual opposites. Hobbes concluded his search for the *purpose* of society by arguing that society is intended to eliminate the ubiquity of violence among men who are not socially organized, and once organized, to control the resort to violence among those who undertake antisocial acts. Although today many sociologists doubt that we can speak of the "purpose" of a social system, they nevertheless parallel Hobbes in arguing that social action in the context of a system *functions* so as to allow the system to exist and persist beyond the life of any one of its members and that a certain sign of the termination of a social system is the return of war among its members. Perfect order in a social system would signify the arrival of utopia; perfect violence would signify the termination of the system (or, as we shall see later, that social behavior had lost all of its systematic quality).

Hobbes's demonstration that society is the conquest of violence rests in part upon a portrayal of what life would be like without society — that is, in the "state of nature." "In such condition there is no place for industry, because the fruit thereof is uncertain: and consequently no culture of the earth; no navigation, nor use of the commodities that may be imported by sea; no commodious buildings; no instruments of moving and removing such things as require much force; no knowledge of the face of the earth; no account of time; no arts; no letters; no society; and which is worst of all, continual fear, and danger of violent death; and the life of man, solitary, poor, nasty, brutish, and short." In order to obtain the fruits of cooperation and the division of labor — which are absent in the state of nature — man must abandon violence. For it is violence, above all else, that characterizes the state of nature: ". . . During the time men live without a common power to keep them all in awe, they are in that condition which is called war; and such a war as is of every man against every man."[10]

Hobbes may have been wrong in thinking that an awesome

power creates the basis for shared expectations, but his insight into the interdependence of order and violence, of society and anarchy, is one of the basic theorems of the sociology of revolution. As Norton Long has observed, "It was the great merit of Hobbes to raise the problems of order — to recognize that the existence of order is problematic."[11] Of course, Hobbes was not the first theorist to perceive this problem. The very roots of Western political philosophy lie in the reaction of some men against the argument that "might makes right" and against man's primitive reliance on force. Some theorists have gone so far as to define the word "political" simply as that element of social organization which is concerned with minimizing and regulating the use of violence.[12]

Since violence is both the negation of, and a possibility in, all social systems, sociologists regard it as one of the major criteria for defining a social system and for evaluating the degree of its stability. Violence differs from the legitimate use of force within a system and even from "routinized" or legally-constrained conflict, such as labor disputes, which may contribute to the functioning of the system, in that violence tends progressively to inhibit and ultimately to extinguish the union of men into a division of labor, regardless of the principles — coercive and/or consensual — which may have been operating to maintain that division of labor. Nevertheless, all social systems are burdened by some degree of violence, either as a consequence of their imperfect integration or due to other functional problems inherent in social organization.

Violence, as we have been talking about it, is still a very broad category of behavior. It may range in form and intensity all the way from gratuitous insults to lunatic acts or criminal behavior directed against other members of the system (e.g., murder or banditry), and from sub-insurrectionary protest movements (such as civil disobedience, politically-motivated fasts and sit-down strikes) to full-fledged rebellion or revolution. Similarly, the effects of violence may vary from a degree of personal tension to the impaired efficiency of large groups of people, and from political instability to the total destruction of the system.

If order and violence are indeed different sides of the same coin, then an analysis of one is inescapably an analysis of the other. This is why the work of Talcott Parsons, who has devoted much attention to the problem of social integration, is of direct relevance to the sociology of revolution (although the present study does not employ any single scholar's theory of integration). It is valuable to recognize, as Lewis Coser has, that "all of Parsons's work, beginning with *The Structure of Social Action,* is an extended commentary on the Hobbesian question: How is social order possible?"[13] On the subject of the relationship between the integration and disintegration of social systems, Parsons himself has written ". . . The maintenance of any existing status [of the social system], insofar as it is maintained at all, is clearly a relatively contingent matter. The obverse of the analysis of the mechanisms by which it is maintained is the analysis of the forces which tend to alter it. *It is impossible to study one without the other.* A fundamental potentiality of instability, an endemic possibility of change, is inherent in this approach to the analysis of social systems. Empirically, of course, the degree of instability, and hence the likelihood of actual change, will vary both with the character of the social system and of the situation in which it is placed. But in principle, propositions about the factors making for maintenance of the system are at the same time propositions about those making for change. The difference is only one of concrete descriptive analysis. There is no difference on the analytical level."[14]

Parsons argues that stability and instability — or, at their extremes, utopia and anarchy — are related configurations in any human grouping and that the analysis of why one condition does or does not prevail is simultaneously the analysis of why its antithesis does or does not prevail. It is for this reason that the amount and nature of violence in a political society have always been regarded as indices either of the society's worth (when viewed by moral philosophers), or of its viability (when viewed by sociologists). Such indices also point up once again the contingent nature of the concept of revolution. Revolution is one form of violence.*

---

* It is instructive to note Lenin's opinion on the possibility of a "nonviolent revolution." In "The Proletarian Revolution and the Renegade Kautsky," he wrote: "Socialism is opposed to violence against nations. That is indisputable. But socialism is opposed to violence against men in general, . . . however, no one has yet drawn the conclusion from this that socialism is opposed to revolutionary violence. Hence, to talk about 'vio-

The general resort to arms or other insurrectionary acts — such as
general strikes, political assassinations, mutinies, and the carrying
out of coups d'état — are all forms of behavior intended to disorient the behavior of others, thereby bringing about the demise
of a hated social system. Changes which occur in society without
the use or threat of violence are nonrevolutionary, and this form
of change is normally preferred to the use of revolutionary violence by men living in society. Normally, socialized men do not
resort to violence except as a last resort (although the perception
of what constitutes a last resort may be colored by an ideology).

If acts of revolutionary violence are quixotic or inappropriate,
they will not be tolerated by other members of the system and
instead of terminating the system they will be dealt with as forms
of crime or lunacy. Acts of revolt "differ from simple crimes to
the extent that collective support given the outlaws is not itself the
product of coercion."[15] Therefore, when revolutionaries promote
and other members of the system accept the return of war, the society itself must have become worse than war; and the desire for
a better society, even at the expense of a temporary return to war,
must have become widespread. True revolution is neither lunacy
nor crime. It is the acceptance of violence in order to cause the
system to change when all else has failed, and the very idea of
revolution is contingent upon this perception of societal failure.

No one has expressed the umbilical connection between revolutionary violence and its social context more succinctly than
Ortega y Gasset: "Man has always had recourse to violence; sometimes this recourse was a mere crime and does not interest us here.
But at other times violence was the means resorted to by him who
had previously exhausted all others in defense of the rights of justice which he thought he possessed. It may be regrettable that human nature tends on occasion to this form of violence but it is
undeniable that it implies the greatest tribute to reason and justice.
For this form of violence is none other than reason exasperated.
Force was, in fact, the *ultima ratio*. Rather stupidly it has been the

lence' in general, without examining the conditions which distinguish
reactionary from revolutionary violence, means being a petty bourgeois
who renounces revolution, or else it means simply deceiving oneself and
others by sophistry." *Selected Works* (New York: International Publishers,
1934-38), VII, 175.

custom to take ironically this expression which clearly indicates the previous submission of force to methods of reason. Civilization is nothing else than the attempt to reduce force to being the *ultima ratio*. We are now beginning to realize this with startling clearness because 'direct action' consists in inverting the order and proclaiming violence as the *prima ratio* or strictly as the *unica ratio*." [16]

The key to both the study and the conceptualization of revolutionary violence lies in social systems analysis. Utilizing the concept of the social system, we can distinguish between those instances of violence within the system that are revolutionary and those that constitute criminal or other forms of violent behavior. Focussing on instances of purposive political violence, we can also use the social system as a reference point for distinguishing between those forms of violence known as war and revolution. Revolution is a form of intrasystemic violence, whereas war is a form of intersystemic violence.

We can also use systems analysis to isolate and compare those instances of purposive political violence that are neither wars nor revolutions. One irreducible characteristic of a social system is that its members hold in common a structure of values. A value structure symbolically legitimates — that is, makes morally acceptable — the particular pattern of interaction and stratification of the members of a social system. By bearing in mind the functions of value structures we can better understand certain kinds of ethnic or intertribal violence that may occur in what is legally a unitary state although, lacking a unified value structure, it is not yet a social system. Instances of such violence have recently been numerous in Africa and southeast Asia and were during the nineteenth century in Europe. As Harry Eckstein has noted: "In the case of the new state . . . there was, in all probability, no previously shared system of norms from which to deviate and, even more probably, no previously settled institutional pattern; there can therefore be no speaking of internal war [revolution] in the proper sense." [17]

The converse of Eckstein's problem is the anomaly discovered by Hannah Arendt that ". . . revolutions, properly speaking, did not exist prior to the modern age; they are among the most recent of all major political data." [18] Social systems analysis is equally instructive here. It is true that pre-modern intrasystemic conflicts were not called "revolutions," but revolutions assuredly occurred prior to the emergence of the nation-state. There were numerous pre-modern social systems in which unified value structures existed but which were not necessarily organized as unitary states (for example, medieval Christendom), and much of the intrasystemic violence that occurred in them should be understood as rebellions or revolutions rather than wars. In some cases this intrasystemic violence may have been closer to routinized conflict than to rebellion or revolution (for example, various medieval wars of succession).

The concept of the value-coordinated social system also helps us to overcome certain errors that result from using Western definitions of violence. It can, for example, solve the puzzle of Max Gluckman's "rituals of rebellion" in Zululand.[19] The violent but routinized behavior of certain factions whenever a new Zulu chieftain was chosen may have been either a ritual or a rebellion, but it cannot very well have been both. If it was a ritual, as seems likely, it constitutes an instance of functional conflict in Zulu society, meeting certain system-derived needs. However, the extraordinary (by Western standards) violence of the behavior has led Gluckman to suggest that the term "rebellion" might be equally appropriate — hence his "rituals of rebellion." But true rebellion is never routinized, being in fact a rejection of old routines; and the determinants of rebellion would be considerably different from the determinants of functional conflict. Again, what is needed is an analysis of the values which allowed Zulus to orient and develop stable expectations toward behavior that in Gluckman's culture is regarded as disorienting and violent.

In this preliminary discussion, it is not being suggested that all insurrections arise from value conflicts. Conflicts over values and conflicts over interests both may produce insurrections, and the distinction between these two kinds of conflict is related to the distinction between rebellions and revolutions. What should be stressed at this point is that any analytical penetration of the behavior characterized as "purposive political violence" must utilize as its prime tool a conception of the social context in which it occurs.

2

The social system:
coercion and values

Wʜᴀᴛ ɪs society? As Dorothy Emmet has ob-
served, society may be "a term meant simply to refer to the concrete fact that a number of people are somehow together, with as
little analytic suggestion as possible as to *how* they are grouped
together." In order to convey this image of society the techniques
of literature, with its emphasis upon immediacy and accuracy, are
most appropriate. "On the other hand, when we talk about a congeries of people as a society, we may be thinking of them as
grouped in virtue of systematic types of relationships, and be trying to exhibit these."[1] Since we are concerned here with analyzing
revolution in the abstract, we need such an abstract conception of
society — one that refers to "some form of empirical alignment
which constitutes a relation between people in virtue of which we
think of them as grouped."[2]

The contemporary idea of a social system, with its subordinate
concepts of role, status, norm, value, structure, functional integration, and so forth, has a distinguished pedigree in the history of
Western political theory. In an analogous form, it is at least as old as

Montesquieu; and its use of the concept of teleological "function," wherein a part is seen as functional insofar as it contributes to the maintenance of a whole, has its logical foundation in Aristotle. However, this idea is also extremely complex. Before introducing all the technical terms which will allow us to talk about the parts of a social system and how they operate, it may be useful to look historically at the dialectical way in which the idea of society as a system has developed.

According to one early and important thesis concerning the nature of society, it is a form of order imposed by some men on others, and maintained by coercion. Hobbes did not hold precisely this view, but he certainly contributed to its development. The major problem to which coercion theorists address themselves is the universal fact of life that all men want more out of their environment than all of them can possibly get. Hobbes has stated the result of this predicament: ". . . If any two men desire the same thing, which nevertheless they cannot both enjoy, they become enemies; and in the way to their end (which is principally their own conservation, and sometimes their delectation [i.e., pleasure] only), endeavor to destroy, or subdue one another."[3] Given the additional Hobbesian assumption that all men are approximately equal in terms of physical strength, the endemic scarcity of goods and the unlimited desires of men account for the perpetual violence of the state of nature. Also this is the impasse which social organization is intended (or functions) to overcome.

Hobbes himself sought to rationalize society by appealing to the common interest men have in avoiding violence. In an organized society, he contends, men will never have all the wealth and prestige they want, but they will receive a stable share and they will be secure from violence in their enjoyment of it. Actually, they have no choice. Given the radical equality among men, should any one attempt to obtain more than his share by resorting to violence against his neighbors, they would respond in kind and all of them would once again return to the state of nature. There, as a consequence of the perpetual violence, they would enjoy even less than they do in the admittedly imperfect state of civil society. The monarch, who is not a party to their "social contract," has more power than any of them; but since he exercises it to control potentially violent men, all men profit from obeying him and from subjecting themselves to him.

Later theorists have been certain that Hobbes was correct in pointing to the fact of universal scarcity and that he was wrong in believing the conflicts generated by it could be eliminated in civil society. Marx, for example, believed that the acquisition of property by some men gave them a power over others which they then used to *enforce* an inherently unequal and therefore unstable order in society. He believed that slowly changing elements in the material environment would erode the original property basis of power and lead to the development of classes and class conflict. A new group of intrinsic possessors, in one epoch the capitalists and in another the proletarians, would then revolt and recast the structure of society in such a way that it reflected and preserved their own interests.

Contemporary coercion theorists continue to believe that the roots of social order lie in the coercion of some men by others, but they have vastly expanded Marx's notion that private property produces an artificial scarcity which generates the need for coercion. In order for men to survive at all in a naturally limited material environment, these theorists argue, people must divide their labor in a stable fashion and provide for the recruitment and assignment of men to various tasks — tasks ultimately dictated by the material environment and of which some will be harder and more important than others.* In order to enforce role assignments, preserve stability in the system, attract specially qualified men through differential rewards, and, in general, enforce the division of labor

* On this point, we may compare the conclusion of David Lockwood: "It is unnecessary to argue that all conflicts, interests, facilities and powers are 'economic' in the sense of being related to the ownership of productive means. . . . The division of labor may be generalized into a category that stands for the factual disposition and organization of socially effective means, and need not be equated simply with the division of functions, powers and interests associated with productive means." "Some Remarks on 'The Social System,'" *British Journal of Sociology*, VII, No. 2 (June 1956), 139. Coercive powers in a society may be held, for example, by a military caste or an ethnic group rather than solely by a propertied class. The only thing that counts, according to this view, is that *some* group has powers over others.

(without which all members of the society would perish or fall to a level of bare subsistence), the division of labor itself demands that some men carry out command and supervisory duties. In order to do this effectively, since there is no natural or rational division of labor among men, coercive powers are necessary; and men must be authorized in some fashion to exercise these coercive powers. As Ralf Dahrendorf, a leading exponent of the coercion theory, has concluded, "The fundamental inequality of social structure, and the lasting determinant of social conflict, is the inequality of power and authority which inevitably accompanies social organization."[4]

This view, if accepted, leads directly to a sociological interpretation of government and to the Weberian theory of the state. Society, conceived as the successful adaptation of a collectivity of people to their environment through a division of their labor, cannot succeed unless some people have power over other people. The need for coercive sanctions rises not simply from the presence of deviants, or fools, or strangers, but from the demands of organization itself. For, although the competition for limited resources may be mitigated to some extent by the division of labor, social organization breeds new interests among men over who should exercise and profit from the powers required by society. This condition gives rise to political conflict and the potential return of violence. The true mark of society, therefore, will be institutions charged with the exercise of physical force both to insure the perpetuation of the division of labor and to regulate the use of violence in conflicts of political interest. The most typical form of such institutions is the state. As Weber put it, "If no social institution existed which knew the use of violence, then the concept of 'state' would be eliminated, and a condition would emerge that could be designated as 'anarchy,' in the specific sense of this word. . . . A state is a human community that (successfully) claims the *monopoly of the legitimate use of physical force* within a given territory. . . . Hence, 'politics' for us means striving to share power or striving to influence the distribution of power, either among states or among groups within a state."[5]

Just as violence was endemic in the Hobbesian state of nature because of scarce means, the threat of violence is endemic in society because of the inequalities in access to power. Marx was right in thinking that social organizations were inherently unstable, but the source of this instability is not changing forces of production but changing relations of power and authority. (The coercion theorists of today reverse Marx's idea that authority is a form of property. They argue that property is, at most, a form of the more general category of authority.)[6] Whether or not the interests generated by the inequalities of coercive capacity will cause the system to erupt into violence ultimately depends upon whether the state's monopoly of power is a genuine monopoly.

In summarizing this view of society, Dahrendorf has written: "From the point of view of coercion theory, . . . it is not voluntary cooperation or general consensus but enforced constraint that makes social organizations cohere. In institutional terms, this means that in every social organization some positions are entrusted with a right to exercise control over other positions in order to ensure effective coercion; it means, in other words, that there is a differential distribution of power and authority. . . . This differential distribution of authority invariably becomes the determining factor of systematic social conflicts of a type that is germane to class conflicts in the traditional (Marxian) sense of the term."[7]

Acknowledging that we have omitted those elements of modern coercion theory that are most damaging to its main premise (e.g., its non-Marxian emphasis upon the legitimation of power and its need to distinguish between latent and manifest interests, points to which we shall return), we may contrast it with its antithesis — the value theory of society. In a sense, the stream of social theorizing that began with Weber and Durkheim and that today is represented by the work of Parsons should be read as a rejoinder to Marx. It does not wholly repudiate the idea that social organization (conceived either materialistically or in terms of the need for coercion) generates its own inequalities and stratification, but it does reject the view that the structure of society is maintained chiefly by the coercion of the many by the power-holding few. Instead, it stresses that society is a "moral community," a collectivity of people who share certain "definitions of the situation" (called "values"), which legitimatize the inequalities of social organization and cause people to accept them as morally justified.

This view contrasts sharply with that of Marx. He was certainly not unaware of the existence of values, but he considered them to be a dependent variable in determining the stability of a particular social order. Values to him were merely the ideological justifications of privilege advanced by the dominant class: ". . . The ruling ideas of a period have always been nothing but the ideas of the ruling class. . . . In each epoch, the thoughts of the ruling class are the ruling thoughts; i.e., the class that is the ruling material power of society is at the same time its ruling intellectual power. The class that has the means of material production in its control, controls at the same time the means of intellectual production."[8] Value theorists, on the other hand, doubt that the ruling beliefs of a society can be reduced to the beliefs of a ruling class; and they explicitly assert that, whatever their origins, values are an independent variable contributing to, or detracting from, the organization and integration of a society.

Parsons, as a leading exponent of this view, is categorical in his rejection of the coercion theory. Instead, he argues that society is not possible unless all the adult members of a society jointly adhere to some principles that render the division of labor intelligible and tolerable. "A relatively established 'politically organized community,'" he writes, "is clearly a 'moral community' to some degree, its members sharing common norms, values, and culture — which is to say that I start with a view that repudiates the idea that any political system that rests *entirely* on self-interest, force, or a combination of them, can be stable over any considerable period of time."[9] In his major work, *The Social System,* Parsons gave his strongest expression to this view: "[The] integration of a set of common value patterns with the internalized need disposition structure of the constituent personalities [i.e., sane, socialized people playing roles in the system] is the core phenomenon of the dynamics of social systems. That the stability of any social system except the most evanescent interaction process is dependent upon a degree of such integration may be said to be the fundamental dynamic theorem of sociology. It is the major point of reference for all analysis which may claim to be a dynamic analysis of social process."[10]

Numerous problems are raised by these two quotations. Are the same values internalized (either through adoption or inculcation)

by all of the members of a system? Or do people agree on values
somewhat in the way that earlier theorists thought people agreed
to "social contracts"? Why do institutions for coercion, such as
the state, exist in societies if everyone agrees on the basis of social
organization? Some of these problems must be delayed until we
discuss the social system in its full complexity and others until
even later when we examine the personal dimensions of systemic
disequilibrium. For the present, let us look somewhat more closely
at the nature of values and how they facilitate men's living together without violence and without an overriding dependence
on coercion.

Values are both *explanations* of a social situation (it does not
matter whether the explanation is causal or mythical) and *standards* of appropriate action designed to produce some desired ("envalued") resolution or management of the situation. They are, for
example, the explanation of why a Hindu outcaste ("untouch-
able") is assigned the miserable tasks that he is in the Indian division
of labor (he has committed a crime in some previous incarnation);
and they tell him, abstractly, how he ought to behave in his present position (accept his lot, thereby preparing the way for an
improved status in a later incarnation). In short, values are social
gestalts or paradigms that, to the extent they are held in common
(i.e., possessed by a group of people who recognize each other
because of their mutual possession of them), lay a foundation of
shared expectations and make possible the orienting of human behavior.

There are many different definitions of values, varying chiefly
according to whether one is interested in the way joint possession
of values produces systematic interactions among people or in the
way an individual person orients his behavior while at the same
time satisfying the demands of his personality. Some approximately
parallel usages include "ideology" in Erik Erikson's sense, both
"culture" and "mazeway" as employed by Anthony Wallace (and
referring, respectively, to the system and to the individual), Sebastian de Grazia's "belief system," Durkheim's *conscience collective,*
Aristotle's principles, or laws, of distributive justice, Carlyle's interpretation of "pagan religion," and the extended sense in which
Hannah Arendt speaks of "authority" and its foundations.

In the more limited realm of organized scientific research,

Thomas Kuhn's "paradigms" are an almost perfect counterpart of values in the society at large. According to Kuhn, paradigms are "universally recognized scientific achievements that for a time provide model problems and solutions to a community of practitioners"; they define what are scientific facts and structure the work of normal science for a particular discipline at a particular time.[11] Talcott Parsons defines values as "the commitments of individual persons to pursue and support certain *directions* or types of action for the collectivity as a system and hence derivatively for their own roles in the collectivity."[12] A definition similar to that of Parsons, stressing commitment but also leaving room for the possible withdrawal of commitment in extremely ambiguous situations, is that of Jacob and his colleagues: values are "the normative standards by which human beings are influenced in their choice among the alternative courses of action which they perceive."[13]

We shall make use of several of these ideas throughout this study. For the moment, let us look at the problem of value sharing and individual human diversity in order to indicate more precisely the ways in which values operate. In a famous and influential article on the "functional prerequisites of a society," D. F. Aberle and others posited that "shared cognitive orientations" were one such prerequisite for the maintenance and continuation of a society.[14] This idea, and similar ones like it derived from Freud, Fromm, Margaret Mead, and Durkheim, created a good deal of confusion in social systems theory when it was confronted with the vast psychoanalytic and behavioral evidence that very few people in a social system actually do share "cognitive orientations" (e.g., motives) to any appreciable degree. Even in a highly homogeneous and physically isolated society whose members may resemble one another in many respects, individuals will persist in thinking their own thoughts and will reveal marked personality differences. How is it possible then for them to hold common values, which cause their behavior to synchronize?

Anthony Wallace has given the most serious attention to this problem. In his opinion the hypothesis that shared cognitive orientations (or thinking alike) are a necessary input into society is erroneous. According to this hypothesis all people in a society are identically motivated and the chief functional problem of a society is the reproduction, through socialization, of people who think alike. Wallace calls this the "replication of uniformity" conception of society and describes it as follows: "If a near-perfect correspondence between culture [including values] and individual nuclear character is assumed, the structural relation between the two becomes non-problematical, and the interest of processual research lies rather in the mechanisms of socialization [child-rearing, education, etc.] by which each generation becomes, culturally and characterologically, a replica of its predecessors. This view is particularly congenial to the world view associated with dynamic psychology, ultimately based on Freud's psychoanalytic theories, but modified by conceiving the personality to reflect faithfully the culture in which it was formed and not merely universal constants, such as the Oedipus conflict and the stages of psycho-sexual maturation."[15]

If the replication of uniformity view were accurate — and it is actually contrary both to common sense experience and to much clinical and statistical evidence — conflict and revolution in a society could have only one cause, namely, the inefficiency or failure of the mechanisms of socialization. In fact, great differences exist among men in terms of their personalities, motives, life experiences, habits, and physical and mental capacities. When these aspects of human diversity are emphasized, Wallace argues, the fundamental problem of an orderly, integrated social system becomes not the replication of uniformity but the "organization of diversity." People do not share motives or cognitive orientations, and value theory does not imply that they must. In fact, if everyone had the same motives, we might doubt that a stable division of labor could exist at all. An identity of motives comes closer to being a premise of the coercion theory, for that theory only makes sense if we assume the existence of identical cognitions, which are rendered incompatible by an environment of scarcity.

What is necessary for a division of labor and for social interaction generally is that "the behavior of other people under various circumstances is predictable, irrespective of knowledge of their motivations, and thus is capable of being predictably related to one's own actions."[16] The sharing of values, or of definitions of a situation, makes this mutual predictability possible. Values are somewhat analogous to final agreements, carefully hammered out in collective bargaining sessions, where precedent, tradition, and universally respected products of inspiration influence the bargainers on all sides. Values establish what Wallace calls "equivalent behavioral expectancies," or, more briefly, "implicit contracts." Using the word "culture" in the sense in which we use the word "value," he concludes: "It is *culture* which is shared (in the special sense of institutional contract) rather than personality, and culture may be conceived as an invention which makes possible the maximal organization of motivational diversity." [17]

As we have seen, two characteristics of values are that they provide people with definitions of situations and with standards of behavior, regardless of their motives. Another characteristic of values is that they constitute symbolic explanations of the human condition. Systems of human action can be distinguished from all other systems in that human beings have a need for believing their actions to be meaningful beyond mere physical maintenance. There are many other problems posed by the individual personality and its particular needs within the context of the social system, and most of these are best delayed until a later stage of analysis; however, a short digression on this subject is unavoidable.

Sometimes we have spoken of the division of labor as if it were the end rather than the beginning of social organization. Actually we know that life in society means a great deal more to its participants than mere cooperative specialization in work or the enslavement of some men by others in order that all may eat. Physical nourishment is one basic human need; but there are other needs which are almost as basic. Past efforts to specify what these needs are have not met with any widespread agreement, but they have led to at least one generalization — namely, that whatever basic human needs there may be, they are arranged hierarchically, and certain needs do not emerge until more basic ones have been fulfilled. An example of such a hierarchy of needs is the one suggested by A. H. Maslow: (a) physical needs (water, food, and sex); (b) safety (order, predictability, and dependability of the environment); (c) love, affection, and belongingness; (d) self-esteem; and (e) self-actualization. [18]

It is not necessary to follow this or any other list of "basic human needs" in order to accept the notion that there is a basic human need for an explanation of the social and material environment in which a human organism finds itself. Presumably this need is of the second order — i.e., on the level of safety in Maslow's list — and emerges together with the appearance of sociopolitical organization in human life. We may explain this need in various ways — e.g., in terms of the positive need for optimism, or hope, in order for people to do more than scavenge for food, or negatively in terms of the inability of people to manage the tension produced by a purposeless existence. The ultimate determinants of such a need probably lie in the greatly increased size of human cranial capacity. Whatever the final cause, people not only divide their labor but also provide themselves with (or accept) some intellectual construct that lends significance to their being together and working together. Values thus provide meanings for social action; they are symbolic interpretations of reality.

Religions, social myths, some moral philosophies, and numerous metaphysical beliefs all contribute to what we have been calling values. Thomas Carlyle, although he seems to have exaggerated wildly both the extent to which the act of myth-making requires "genius" and the extent to which it is deserving of being worshipped as "heroic," understood better than most social scientists the need men have for myths. In his own, ultra-distinctive style, he wrote: "Pagan religion is indeed an Allegory, a Symbol of what men felt and knew about the Universe; and all Religions are Symbols of that, altering always as that alters: but it seems to me a radical perversion, and even *in*version, of the business, to put that forward as the origin and moving cause, when it was rather the result and termination. To get beautiful allegories, a perfect poetic symbol, was not the want of men; but to know what they were to believe about this Universe, what course they were to steer in it; what, in this mysterious Life of theirs, they had to hope and to fear, to do and to forbear doing."[19]

Carlyle recognized intuitively that the possession of a mythical or causal explanation of life is one of the attributes of socialized human beings. Unfortunately, such explanations are not, as he contends, "altering always as that [the life situation] alters." Sometimes they do change in relative synchronization with the environment of a society, and it is greatly to the advantage of social stability that they do so. At other times, however, they may change without the empirical situation having changed at all (for example, as a result of cultural borrowings or innovations in scientific paradigms); or they may remain unchanged while the empirical situation is being transformed (for example, as a result of technical innovation or the corrupt exploitation of a government). These circumstances of noncongruence pose the greatest threat to the stability and ultimate viability of a social system. Values, in the present sense of symbolic interpretations of reality, are governed by a principle rather analogous to that of the state conceived as a monopoly of force; both had better maintain their monopolies if they are not to be subverted and, possibly, overthrown. It is for this reason, as we shall see, that the explanatory, or definitional, function of values has such great relevance to the sociology of revolution.

With regard to the organization of the division of labor, values obviate the need to rest the inescapable discriminations among the supply of talents and the demands of environmental adaptation primarily upon coercion.[20] For example, in societies that possess values which establish competition and achievement as the just way to recruit individuals into the more desirable duties, the resulting stratification of winners and losers is made morally acceptable to both strata. It is not necessary to force the losers' stratum to perform the systemically-acknowledged less desirable jobs, for the value systems of such societies will include compensatory values for the losers. "The meek shall inherit the earth," the myth of the Noble Poor, and popular beliefs that contrast the responsibilities of the powerful with the freedom of the unencumbered illustrate such compensatory values. In a similar fashion, societies with ascriptive values do not generate conflict when the eldest son of a ruler succeeds his father; and they normally tolerate, or systematically compensate for, the inefficiency that results if the son does not possess the temperament of a good ruler. As these examples also illustrate, the types of values a society has provide the basis for a typology of societies.

The most important function of the value system in a society is to authorize, or legitimatize, the use of force. Although the distinction between power and authority is almost as old as political theory itself, the precise relationship between the use of force and the two facets of this behavior known as "power" and "authority" remains imprecise in social systems analysis. Too often social theorists have merely followed Weber, who defined power as the "probability that one actor within a social relationship will be in a position to carry out his own will despite resistance, regardless of the basis on which this probability rests," and authority as "the probability that a command with a given specific content will be obeyed by a given group of persons."[21] This distinction leads directly to the rather misleading conclusion that "the important difference between power and authority consists in the fact that whereas power is essentially tied to the personality of individuals, authority is always associated with social positions or roles. . . . While power is merely a factual relationship, authority is a legitimate relation of domination and subjection."[22]

Translated into value theory, such a distinction between power and authority is roughly the same as the distinction between the state of nature and the value-coordinated moral community. As Weber well knew, however, both power and authority exist — concretely and conceptually — within a moral community. What is needed, therefore, is a threefold distinction between strength, power, and authority. In the state of nature — an ideal realm of human interaction not coordinated by shared values — strength is the touchstone in determining the outcome of any instance of social conflict. We may conceive of this strength as relatively equally distributed among men, as Hobbes did, and argue that violence is therefore a continuous phenomenon in the state of nature, unrelieved by the domination of one man over others. Or we may argue that even in the state of nature one armed man or a group of kinsmen can establish some order through the coercion of others. In either case, however, such relationships are mediated by a calculus of strength (including the effect of strength to create some order through deterrence), and strength is always a personal characteristic of the dominant party. Questions of legitimacy play no part whatsoever in this pure calculus of strength.*

* This distinction between strength and power is identical to that of Hannah Arendt: "In distinction to strength, which is the gift and the possession of every man in his isolation against all other men, power comes

Power and authority, on the other hand, both refer to relationships of legitimacy, the first being a generalized kind of legitimate relationship and the second being a highly specific institution charged with regulating tests of legitimacy when they occur and exercising physical coercion in order to preserve the division of labor. Let us try to elucidate the differences between these two concepts within a value-coordinated system. In a stable social system, as we have seen, the members share values which permit them, through mutual expectations, to orient their behavior. That is to say, value sharing establishes a degree of trust and confidence in the normalcy of a particular pattern of social interaction and in the likelihood of its continuing. This trust, which is a characteristic of all moral communities, permits members greatly to expand their activities because they do not have to make continuous appeals to supervisory and commanding organs for decisions. In a moral community most of the fundamental questions of how to organize social action have been settled, at least temporarily, and members can therefore get on with the daily business of life as it is lived in that particular context.

Within such communities, the expansion and proliferation of activities are not random. They are carried out in conformity with what Parsons calls "generalized [i.e., standardized] media of the interaction process," which may also be understood as alternative but complementary regulators of behavior, or techniques of social control.[23] All these media rest in major degree upon the trust and confidence generated by value sharing. Parsons suggests that there are four types of social control, each one utilizing specific media of interaction. They are: (a) the offer of positive advantages, or inducement, using the media of economic exchange (e.g., a monetary system); (b) the invocation of obligations, or power, using the media that threaten disadvantage (e.g., coercion); (c) the use of persuasion, or influence; and (d) the appeal to conscience, or the direct invocation of the moral standards of right and wrong within a value system.

into being only if and when men join themselves together for the purpose of action, and it will disappear when, for whatever reason, they disperse and desert one another." *On Revolution* (New York: Viking Press, 1963), p. 174.

It is not necessary for us to argue here that this list is exhaustive or that it could not be formulated in some other way. We are satisfied that it conceptualizes a phenomenon easily observed empirically: that communities in which trust and confidence prevail systematically enlarge the number of interactions and the produce of the division of labor many times over that which exists in coercive communities. The idea directly relevant to studies of violence is that power is one generalized medium of interaction. In order to illustrate its properties as a medium of interaction and to stress its reliance on the trust and confidence of value-coordinated societies, Parsons compares power to another generalized medium — money.

A basic theorem in economics and a concrete principle in the daily operations of central banks is that "the primary basis of the value of money is general confidence that expectations of the productivity of the system will be realized."[24] Power, as a generalized medium, operates in a way analogous to the functioning of money. "The money held by a social unit is, we may say, the unit's capacity, through market channels under given rules of procedure, to command goods and services in exchange, which for its own reasons it desires. Correspondingly, the power of a unit is its capacity, through invoking binding obligations [e.g., civic obligations such as military service, contractual obligations, the obligation to follow vested leadership, and so forth] to contribute to collective goals, to bring about collective goal-inputs that the 'constituents' of the collective action in question desire. . . . Once units are brought within the relevant context of collective organization, power is the medium of invoking their obligations to contribute to collective functioning. . . . [Like monetary systems, power systems] depend on the continuing willingness of their members to entrust their status in and interpretations of the collective interest to an impersonal process in which binding decisions are made without the members being in a position to control them [directly]."[25]

Amounts of power and money are greatly expandable in systems wherein the mediation of values generates conditions of trust and confidence. But the viability of neither power nor money rests solely on trust. There will always be some people, for reasons to be explained later, who refuse to obey invocations of obligations or accept legal tender or bank drafts. In the first instance, those who exercise power resort to imposing progressively greater disadvantages (negative sanctions), just as the authors of rejected bank drafts either arrange to pay increasing amounts of their debts in monetized bullion or reduce their debts by contracting economic operations. However, "the question of whether [force] is or is not the 'basis' of power is ambiguous in a sense exactly parallel to that of the question of 'basing' the value of money on command of gold reserves." [26] Trust in the system itself is as important in the operation of these media as are the supplies of either force or gold. And it is the joint possession of a value system (in the specific sense of shared "culture") that lays the ultimate foundation of trust.

Since occasionally there will be "deflations" in the power system, similar to monetary deflations, society needs institutions authorized to exercise force in order to reestablish confidence. The most typical form of this institution is the state. The state is the institutionalization of *authority*, which is a special form of power. Authorities may themselves invoke obligations (exercise power), but if they are not obeyed they may also use force in order to ensure compliance. Moreover, since they maintain a monopoly over the use of force they are the final appeal for individuals lacking the authority to use force, whose exercise of power has met with a negative response. Roles entrusted with authority are keepers of the *ultima ratio*, but they do not exercise all power within a system. The concentration of all power and all authority in the hands of the government would be, in fact, an ideal definition of totalitarianism. In the stable, value-sharing community, the distribution of power produces a relatively much higher level of effective collective action than in the tyrannous state, or in the state so oriented toward a single goal that the totalitarian form of organization becomes tolerable.

The value system defines the roles and statuses of authority, and at the same time is the source of this authority's legitimacy. When force is used by authorities in a manner understood or expected by those sharing the system of values — i.e., in a way to which all value-sharers are committed — it is said to be legitimate. Any other use of force, including that by persons who exercise power but not authority, is condemned as violence and is itself subject to a negative obligation (exercise of power) and to suppression by legitimate force (exercise of authority).

The capacity of authorities to maintain confidence in the power system does not, of course, rest solely on the use of force; that only becomes true in the last resort. The possession of a true monopoly over the legitimate use of force allows the authorities to exercise control through coercion, of which the use of force is only the final and extreme form in a hierarchy of means. Coercion includes deterrence by threat or warning, the prevention of actions by means of physical confinement, other forms of punishment (e.g., fining), a symbolic demonstration of the capacity to act by the maintenance of superior means of force, and, finally, the use of force itself.[27] Since one of the purposes (or functions) of the value-coordinated social system is to release communal energies through the generation of confidence (or stable expectations), the use of force in the exercise of authority is rare and carefully circumscribed. If it is used capriciously, even though the commander of the force may be authorized to use it by the concrete rules of the system (the distinction between rules, or norms, and values will be introduced later), this use of force will be disorienting and condemned as violence (a military coup d'état is an extreme example). Legitimacy is a function of the value structure, not a carte blanche for the occupants of certain statuses to compel obedience to their orders.

Since this threefold distinction between strength, power, and authority covers a greater range of behavior than is generally included under the Weberian definitions of power and authority, it is particularly useful for conceptualizing dysfunctional and potentially revolutionary conditions in the value-coordinated social system. The prime characteristic of revolutionary conditions, in the opinion of many political theorists, is the "loss of authority." Hannah Arendt, for example, has written, "No revolution ever succeeded, [and] few rebellions ever started, so long as the authority of the body politic was truly intact."[28] In a different context, she has concluded, "Generally speaking, we may say that no revolution is even possible where the authority of the body politic is truly intact, and this means, under modern conditions, where the armed forces can be trusted to obey the civil authorities."[29]

At a later point we shall explore in detail the ramifications of the "loss of authority." However, simply in terms of our present distinctions, we can see that it implies above all a "power deflation." Ever-increasing demands for the use of the *ultima ratio* as well as a great contraction of the political capacity of a system are, empirically, danger signals indicating the proximity of revolution. When confidence has evaporated to the extent that the exercise of power is futile, when the authority of the status-holders entrusted with supervision and command rests *only* on their monopoly of force, and when there is no forseeable prospect of a processual change in this situation, revolution is at hand. Since superior strength is now the sole basis for social order, there will usually be an increase in the strength of the police and army.* Such superior force may delay the eruption of violence; nevertheless, a division of labor maintained by Cossacks is no longer a community of value-sharers, and in such a situation (e.g., South Africa today), revolution is endemic and, *ceteris paribus*, an insurrection is inevitable. This fact reveals once again the necessity of investigating a system's value structure and its problems in order to conceptualize the revolutionary situation in any theoretically meaningful way.

Sociological value theory explicitly rejects the notion that social cooperation is coerced; in its conception of a system's integration, the authoritative or legitimate use of force is limited to situations where the consensus on values has broken down and, even then, only as a last resort. The question raised by this kind of value theory is why institutions of authority should be needed

---

* The conclusion of Stanislaw Andrzejewski offers a comparison: "Government not based on naked force can function only if certain beliefs are accepted by the overwhelming majority of the population; if there is an agreement on the right to command and duty to obey. If such agreement does not exist, either because of ethnic heterogeneity or in consequence of an internal schism, naked force must remain the argument of last resort, and the distribution of military might the principal determinant of social structure." *Military Organization and Society* (London: Routledge & Kegan Paul, 1954), p. 123.

at all in a community based upon value sharing, in which the basic questions of justice and equity have been settled. Why do some men withdraw their commitment to a system's values? Why do some people refuse to obey invocations of obligation or accept bank drafts? Why, in short, do "power deflations" sometimes occur?

Contemporary value theorists address themselves to this problem chiefly through the concept of "deviant behavior" (i.e., deviant from the point of view of the standards prescribed by a value system). According to value theorists, the major causes of deviancy within the value-coordinated division of labor are three: (a) imperfect socialization, meaning that the values of the system have been imperfectly imparted to new members; (b) "role strain," resulting from the attempt to integrate one system (the human being), with its own needs, into another system (the society). This can lead to socially caused mental illness, in which the demands of some roles conflict with some individuals' personality needs to produce defensive deviant reactions, such as neurotic withdrawal or aggression; and (c) normative dissensus, resulting from conflicting norms or ambiguities within the value system itself — for example, the dilemma of the physician who is committed to relieving the suffering of rich and poor alike in a system which also values the acquisition of wealth through profit taking.[30]

These are extremely important sources of potential conflict, violence, and even revolt; and they are sufficient in themselves to warrant institutions of authority to enforce social behavior. However, it is extremely dangerous and misleading to conceive of the sources of antisocial behavior (and the need for coercive institutions) only in this way. From the point of view of the logic of value theory, these kinds of deviancy could all, in principle, be eliminated from the social system. They are not generated by the structure of society itself, but by imperfections in the structure — e.g., by unstandardized socialization procedures, imperfect role assignments, or inconsistencies in legal and normative codes. Efficient social engineering, such as that envisaged by Aldous Huxley in his *Brave New World*, could eliminate these flaws and thereby eliminate the need for the state.

The greatest weakness of value theory, when it is used as the *sole* analytical tool in conceptualizing the social system, is its inability to conceive of any form of antisocial behavior other than deviancy. This becomes more evident when we push the implications of value sharing to their extremes. Unalloyed value theory, as it was conceived by some nineteenth century writers, provides the basis for the ideal of the historical Anarchist movement and for Marx's vision of true communism. As the Anarchist writer, Anselme Bellegarrigue, stated in 1848: "Anarchy is order, government is civil war."[31] Few social scientists today would equate anarchy with order, since to them anarchy means the condition in which social actors hold incompatible and incongruous definitions of a situation of social action.[32] To the Anarchists, however, the word meant precisely the opposite.

Wilhelm Weitling, for example, as quoted by Bakunin, said: "The perfect society has no government, only an administration, no laws only obligations, no punishments only means of correction."[33] And how is this society to be achieved? The answer is obvious. So long as men agree on the need for an equitable division of labor and on their mutual interests in cooperation and obligations to cooperate with each other (i.e., so long as they share the same values), coercive institutions become unnecessary and even pernicious. Seen from the Anarchist perspective, authority appears in a new light: it is the devilishly clever instrument of exploitation used by a truly antisocial ruling class.

Pure value theory is only slightly dissimilar. It takes a tragic view of authority, arguing that it is an inescapable consequence of man's imperfectibility, a necessary antidote to "deviancy." That Anarchism and an extreme statement of value theory do coincide is strongly suggested by Proudhon's answer to the question, "What guarantees the observance of justice [in Anarchist society]?" "The same thing that guarantees that the merchant will respect the coin — faith in reciprocity, that is to say, justice itself. Justice is for intelligent and free beings the supreme cause of their decisions."[34]

What is wrong with these views? Why should so powerful a tool of social analysis as value theory lead to such an absurd conclusion? The answer is that value theory is unable to conceive of sources of interest and conflicts of interest other than the interest men have in conforming to a value system's definition of a situation. A fully articulated model of the social system must therefore go beyond simple value theory and supplement it with an analysis of nonnormative conflict occurring in and having an effect on the value-coordinated social system.

As we have seen, value sharing makes possible an expansion of collective action well beyond the level of coerced cooperation, but values and the people united by them never exist in a vacuum. A system of social action has for its setting a complex social, economic, and political environment (i.e., an economic geography and the presence of other, often hostile, social systems). The values of the system are, so to speak, addressed to this "environment," and they can either facilitate or retard attempts to exploit and adapt to it. Values themselves cannot be *derived* entirely from the existential determinants of societies, except within the broadest limits (e.g., the values appropriate to a peasant society would be dysfunctional among hunters and gatherers); but values do interact (and hopefully synchronize) with a concrete sociopolitical environment. The influence of the environment — the "substratum" of social action, or the tangible facts of life which the value structure explains and makes intelligible — must be considered on a par with that of the value system in any analysis of the determinants of a particular social system.

Values and the requirements of environmental adaptation determine a social structure; they also produce conflicts within it. As we indicated earlier, social organization has as its primary purpose (or function) the maintenance of order, or the transcendence of violence. Violence (in the sense of a purposive strategy of violence, or more generally, any form of behavior to which people are unable to orient themselves) is caused by *relations of conflict*. These relations of conflict are, in Dahrendorf's definition, "all relations between sets of individuals that involve an incompatible difference of objective."[35] In order to reduce the amount of violence among its members, a social system must eliminate some relations of conflict and "routinize" others — that is, envelop them in rules accepted by both sides so that the relationship becomes competitive (a "game") and not disorienting.

Certainly all social conflict does not lead to violence; it is often an agreed-upon method for reaching decisions without violence (e.g., collective bargaining), and much of it contributes to the maintenance of the system.* However, any relationship involving conflict can lead to violence, and the extent to which a system eliminates or routinizes relations of conflict is therefore a measure of its viability (one possible cause of its demise being the return of the war of all against all).

Relations of conflict uniformly resolved by violence are ubiquitous in the state of nature. Relations of conflict resolved by means other than violence are ubiquitous in society. A specific value system synchronized with a specific pattern of environmental adaptation (i.e., a division of labor that copes with its particular socioeconomic terrain) inescapably gives rise to conflicts at the same time that it provides the means for eliminating or routinizing them. The problem of social conflict and its resolution cannot be understood unless both the value and environmental *sources* of conflict are considered and unless the conflict-regulating *capacity* of a system is considered in the context of the way in which its values legitimatize the particular arrangements by which the system adapts to its environment.

We have already mentioned some of the conflicts which the value system itself may generate (i.e., those caused by faulty socialization, role strain, and normative dissensus). The environment also generates conflicts. One form of these, conflicts of interest, stems from the competition for scarce goods. Value sharing mitigates these conflicts to some extent, but never eliminates them entirely. The value system may cause people to accept

---

* Weber's distinctions on these points are helpful: "A social relationship will be referred to as 'conflict' in so far as action within it is oriented intentionally to carrying out the actor's own will against the resistance of the other party or parties. The term 'peaceful' conflict will be applied to cases in which actual physical violence is not employed. A peaceful conflict is 'competition' in so far as it consists in a formally peaceful attempt to attain control over opportunities and advantages which are also desired by others. A competitive process is 'regulated' competition to the extent that its ends and means are oriented to an order." *The Theory of Social and Economic Organization* (New York: The Free Press of Glencoe, paperbound ed., 1964), pp. 132-33.

the broad differentials in rewards among social strata, but conflicts of interest will still be generated among individuals or groups occupying the same stratum and in the processes of exchange between strata. In order to prevent these conflicts of material interest from leading to violence, the system will derive norms of bargaining and compromise from the overall value structure. If these norms prove unequal to the resolution of such conflicts, thereby generating further disagreements (this time over "the normative status of social objects"),[36] the conflicts must then be presented to the authorities for their action. They can resolve the conflicts either by deciding them on the basis of existing laws or norms, or by legislating new and more acceptable laws. Whatever they decide, they may have to enforce their decisions by the use of force. The existence of these sorts of conflicts thus demands that the society entrust certain roles with authority; and the stability of the society will depend, in one measure, upon the success of its authorities in "routinizing" the acceptance of their decisions and in preventing some conflicts from developing through the routine reform of norms.

Another environmental source of conflict is created by the successful management of the first. The very fact that relationships of power and authority do exist in a system creates the basis for conflicts of political interest. Power and authority, by definition, involve relationships of command and obedience — that is, of inequality. The presence of power thus automatically initiates a competition among men to become the possessor of it, and these political conflicts may become violent. The value system will eliminate certain of the conflicts by providing jointly understood definitions of the type of man who ought to occupy a particular power position. It will attempt to routinize the remaining conflicts by articulating rules for regulating, or institutionalizing, the competition for power. If, however, men who enjoy power betray the values of the system by employing violence, either in the process of acquiring or occupying a power status, an attempt will be made by other power holders to punish them for their behavior through the use of legitimate force. If the betrayal cannot be rectified, it may produce a rebellion.

Still a third form of social conflict is interstratum disputes,

which often concern both the distribution of scarce goods and
the allegedly excessive powers of the ruling stratum (e.g., "class
warfare"). The value structure plays a crucial role in preventing
such conflicts. It explains and legitimatizes the stratification of the
system and, at the same time, attempts to reduce the likelihood of
interstratum conflict by developing norms such as equal opportunity, social mobility, co-option, and philanthropy. When conflicts do develop, the authorities must take action to relieve them.
The only remedy for this kind of conflict relationship is social
change of either the value structure, or the pattern of the division
of labor, or both, in order to bring them back into synchronization. During the time that this change is being accomplished,
a power deflation is likely to develop, requiring the use of force
to maintain order in the system. If the authorities fail to recognize
these situations or fail by their actions to correct them, other
things being equal, a revolution will ensue.

Conflict theorists acknowledge the role of value sharing in reducing the likelihood of interstratum conflicts of interest. They
do this through a distinction between "latent and manifest interests."[37] Latent interests, a purely analytical construct, refer to the
interests any player of a subordinate role, or occupant of a subordinate status (or groups of such people), *might* have if the
value system did not make his position in the hierarchy acceptable.
Manifest interests, or what Marx called "class consciousness,"
refer to the interests in preserving or altering a *status quo* that are
self-consciously perceived by persons who are parties to an interstratum relationship of conflict. According to this distinction,
latent interests will never become manifest so long as the value
structure remains synchronized with the demands of environmental adaptation. If they do become manifest, the society must
either change in the direction of resynchronization or explode into
violent revolution. The actions of the authorities are obviously
central in determining which alternative will occur.

In considering whether or not relations of conflict will lead to
social violence, the main dynamic condition we must explore is
the synchronization between the value system and the division of
labor. Values and the division of labor are both independent variables determining this condition. It is not enough to study either

the one or the other, or both separately; values and the circumstances of environmental adaptation must both be studied with regard to the way in which each does, or does not, complement the other. David Lockwood has expressed the reasoning behind this approach as follows: "Just as the problem of order is not just a function of the existence of a normative order and the social mechanisms which procure motivation to conform with it [e.g., socialization] but also of the existence of a social substratum [division of labor] which structures interests differentially in the social system, so the problem of conflict is not reducible to the analysis of the division of labor and the group interests consequent on it. It is rather that both conflict and order are a function of the interaction of norm and substratum."[38] In order to conceptualize these relationships, we need a model of the social system that synthesizes the coercion theory and the value theory of social integration. Such a model provides the key to analyzing the changing society — one that may be threatened with revolution.

3

The social system:
structure and function

We began the last chapter by asking "What is society?" Now we shall rephrase this question using the more analytical language of social science and ask "What is a social system?" The word "system," when properly used, describes any group of variables which are so arranged that they form a whole (e.g., a solar system) and which have a particular kind of relationship with each other — namely, they are mutually influencing ("interdependent") and they tend to maintain the relationship they have with each other over time ("equilibrium").[1] Because human societies often display these characteristics, social scientists have found it intellectually profitable to conceive of the order displayed by human societies as a "systematic" type of order. In studying the systematic order of human societies, we must specify, on the one hand, the variables which are interdependent and which constitute the structure of social action and, on the other hand, the work these variables must perform in order to create and maintain an equilibrium, or what is sometimes called the functional prerequisites of a social system.

In this book we are not interested in all human situations that could be described as social systems or subsystems (e.g., churches, armies, families), but only in those social systems that constitute whole human societies. The defining characteristics of such societies are that they: (a) exist longer than the life-span of any one individual contributing to them; (b) form self-sufficient wholes; and (c) replenish their supplies of contributing actors, at least in part, through sexual reproduction.[2] Our problem, therefore, is to describe analytically the parts, their interdependence, and the equilibrium of a self-reproducing, self-sufficient system of human behavior that persists beyond the life-span of any one member.

The parts that constitute a social system of cooperative action are patterns of behavior to which members of the system are oriented by virtue of such patterns of behavior being expected. They are the tasks which are divided up and assigned in the division of labor, and they are known as roles. No man's life is taken up entirely with maintaining or reproducing the system of social action he belongs to, but all actions that have any significance from the perspective of the social system (the perspective taken by the systems analyst) are actions in conformity with, or in violation of, a role. Role analysis is the study of the consequences, intentional or unintentional, for the maintenance of the total system, of a particular ensemble of roles and of the ways in which they are performed.

The idea of role does not depend upon the motivation of the person who is playing one. Role is a concept which should be understood in terms of Wallace's "organization of diversity" image of society. As David Riesman has observed, "Roles within a social system may harness various types of personalities. To put it more specifically, you can get the same kind of political behavior, for instance, out of quite different human types. Although the behavior has different meanings for these people, the understanding of their differences and those different meanings may be quite irrelevant to their political and public role."[3] A player of a role may understand his role simply as a series of obligations and rights which are socially recognized and which, being so recognized, allow him to determine his own behavior and to orient himself to the behavior of others.

Behavior in roles is sometimes institutionalized. An institution-alized role is either one whose rules of performance have been codified or made legally explicit (with specific sanctions attached for nonperformance) – e.g., a tax collector – or a role whose standards of performance are so widely known and agreed upon throughout the society that only relatively limited variations in execution are allowed – e.g., the roles inherent in the institution of marriage and the family. Institutions may also refer to sets of roles whose standardized expectations of behavior have been made explicit – e.g., a government bureaucracy.

No role is absolutely rigid in its standards of performance. Even a constitutionally-defined role such as Supreme Court justice has changed as a result of conscious innovations and the way in which various incumbents have differed in their performances of the role, even though the role requirements have remained the same.[4] However, variations in the performance of roles can never be entirely separated from the way in which a role is defined by the social system regardless of who may be the role incumbent. "Role requirements . . . constitute ranges of tolerable behavior rather than highly precise behavioral limitations. Extremes will normally be subject to negative sanctions, with considerable lati-tude in between."[5]

Role requirements, or standards of expected performance which govern roles, are norms. They are positive rules of behavior, ap-propriate to a particular role, which are elaborated in accordance with a system's value structure; and they may be created through codification or inherited from custom, or both. Codified norms control institutionalized roles. A common way in some societies to institutionalize a role or role set is to codify its norms through a legitimate, authoritatively-enforced, legal system (e.g., military roles are codified in most nation-states today, but they depended on custom in most feudal societies). Values, as we have seen, differ from norms in that they are the general moral and definitional symbols which, when shared, establish the conscious solidarity that characterizes men joined together in a moral com-munity. Thus the value of "private property" or "freedom of expression" is given normative expression by specific rules that say what kinds of social transactions and events should be sanctioned in order to realize such values. The concrete rules of behavior attached to various roles (e.g., the taboo against incest, or the legal and customary obligations controlling economic exchange) and the institutionalized sets of norms which guide the allocation and assignment of roles of authority (e.g., political constitutions) are inspired and legitimatized by the system's value structure. Since values themselves interact with the demands of environmental adaptation, norms derived from a value structure will provide morally acceptable (i.e., legitimate) rules for performing the roles dictated by a particular division of labor.

The efficiency of norms in controlling role behavior is particularly sensitive to the degree of complementarity that exists between the value structure and the environment. In societies in which the two are almost perfectly synchronized, the rules of behavior will hardly appear to be rules at all, and the enactment of new rules will be the result of political consensus more than the outcome of political conflict. In societies in which values and the division of labor are dissynchronized, norms, and particularly institutionalized norms, will have a much higher degree of saliency. At times when values are insecure as a result of social change, norms themselves — partially legitimatized by the crumbling value structure but also buttressed by coercive enforcement — become the basic principles for organizing the work of the society. Since they no longer rest on a solid basis of legitimacy in shared values, norms in times of change will be subject to frequent violations, taxing the abilities of authorities to enforce them; and their contents will become a major focus of attention and argument in the society. In stable times, by contrast, norms are accepted unquestioningly as envalued definitions of the environment.

In addition to having roles and norms governing these roles, a society must differentiate between the various activities required by its values and environment in such a way that a workable ensemble of roles exists. Age and sex differences alone impose a degree of natural role differentiation on any society, and no single man can perform all of the roles of his society through his own labor, no matter how simple the tasks required.[6] However, in differentiating among roles, assigning people to them, settling conflicts of interest based on scarcity, and solving the disputes arising from multiple role playing and role confusion (e.g., the concrete problems posed by one man playing the roles of legislator and businessman, and the systemic problems posed by the conflicting roles of priest and scientist), the society must entrust some roles with supervisory powers and with the authority to enforce decisions. As we saw in the last chapter, conflicts of interest over the differential rewards attached to various roles create a primary need for authority. The existence of authority itself creates further conflicts of political interest which require still more managerial and supervisory roles capable of exercising coercive authority.

The inevitable result of solving problems of role differentiation, role assignment, and conflict resolution is the creation of a rank-order, or hierarchy, of roles. The basis of the hierarchy is a value-derived determination of the importance of each role, and the product is a stratified system of roles in which various classes of roles carry different amounts of prestige. The position occupied by each role within a network of stratification is called its status.

Status is the structural, or architectonic, dimension of the dynamic concept of role. A status is a social position endowed with certain rights and obligations, whereas the exercise of these rights and obligations by the occupant of the status is the performance of his role. Like role, status is a social concept; a person cannot occupy a status or play a role all by himself.[7] Since each status, as well as the whole network of stratification, is legitimatized by the value structure, and since a system of roles must also come to grips with the realities of a society's environment, the stability of the status hierarchy is a function of the degree of synchronization that exists between the value structure and adaptation to the environment. Similarly, the inputs into the value-environmental nexus establish the limits within which the particular configuration of a given status hierarchy may vary (e.g., merchants always occupy low statuses in peasant societies, but their precise status varies among peasant societies). Status and role are, respectively, the static and dynamic aspects of the basic concept of the division of labor. Value explanations and definitions of the division of labor make the discriminations between various statuses morally acceptable. However, to the extent that the value structure fails to render legitimate the hierarchy of stratification, status protests will develop, threatening the entire status structure and leading potentially to a recasting of the division of labor.

Using the ideas of role, norm, and status, we are able to conceptualize the structural nature of a system of social action. A social system is composed of actions (roles), played from statuses and guided by norms. As Dahrendorf has put it, "The basic unit of structural analysis . . . is that of role, i.e., a complex of behavioral expectancies which are associated with a given social position or status. In structural analysis, the human individual in the fullness of his expressions figures only as an incumbent of such positions, and 'player' of roles."[8] A structure, however, is not a system; a system has a structure. Once we have stated what a system's structure is, we are still left with the complex question of how this structure functions to meet the needs of the system (determined by value and environmental interaction) and to maintain an equilibrium.

The phrase "to meet the needs of the system" raises one of the truly controversial questions in the history of social analysis. The very word "needs" implies the question "needs for what?" What are the ends of a social system that generate a need to reach, or fulfill, them? To suggest that social systems have needs is to imply that social systems have ends. Yet many political philosophers and most social scientists deny that the ends of society are, or can be, known by human beings. Today, in fact, most social scientists reject the notion that a social system has any end — in the sense of a purpose or an intention — at all.

True, actors or groups within a social system do have ends. As Emmet points out: "Politics is . . . a signal example of an activity in which those who engage in it will talk and think in terms of purpose; and when we are meaning by 'politics' political science as the study of this activity, we shall need sometimes at any rate to put questions in purposive terms and to ask what people are trying to do when they act politically, or what they have set up some particular institution for." There is nothing illogical about such research, and we shall utilize this approach in a later chapter. It is perfectly appropriate to ask human beings what their purposes, or ends, are when we are attempting to make statements about the causes of their actions. However, it is not appropriate to ask a social system the same question; a system of social action does not have a "general will" and cannot have a purpose in the same way a human being can. Emmet reminds us that ". . . the classical tradition in political theory was written in terms of the notion of 'the purpose of the state,' and the purposes of particular institutions within it, and so under-estimated the part played by customs whose unintended but socially important consequences are better studied in functional terms."[9]

When we make a causal statement about an individual's actions in terms of the ends he has in mind we are engaging in a form of teleological reasoning — i.e., reasoning in which "a *future* event which has not yet happened must be named among the causal factors of a present event."[10] According to modern scientific logic, the only valid form of teleological reasoning is the conscious teleology of purposeful action by a human being; however, some logicians would still prefer a nomological explanation of human action (i.e., an explanation in terms of antecedent events and general laws), and they argue that this is possible if we regard the actor's motives as antecedent events. Since social systems, as systems, demonstrably do not have purposes or motives in the way a reasoning organism does, many social scientists have totally rejected that tradition of political philosophy which speaks of the purposes of the state or society. They point out that this kind of theory has been forced to make its final argument the existence of some metaphysical person, such as God, who could have a purpose. These theorists insist that the only kind of valid explanation of a social event, or of any other event for that matter, is a historical one. Unfortunately, historians have yet to discover a single social law, and we are still a long way from a nomological social science.

Taking a cue from the biological sciences, social science has attempted to overcome this dilemma by reintroducing a modified form of teleological reasoning — namely, the logic of "functionalism." Using the concept of function, we can talk about the "purpose" of a part within a system even when we do not know, or doubt, that it has a conscious purpose. Functional logic has

been a great boon to anthropologists, for example, in studying primitive societies. These societies often had institutionalized behavior that was incomprehensible from the point of view of the experiences of the Western-trained anthropologist. When the cultural anthropologist asked questions about the purpose of a funeral, a potlatch, a sacrifice, or a puberty rite in such a society, he usually received an answer that left him as mystified as before he had asked. Only through careful analysis of the particular social system in which the behavior occurred could he say what function the behavior served for the "ends" of the system.*
As Emmet has remarked, "The 'function' may be the unintended consequence of something which people think they are doing for some quite different reason, or may have no clear idea of the reason for which they are doing it. . . . What can be stated in terms of the functional concepts, but not in terms of purposive ones, are the consequences of people's actions which work out in a way which helps maintain a form of society without their being intended to do so."[11]

Emmet's last sentence is crucial to the logical integrity of functional analysis. Functionalism is a kind of non-purposive teleology and, as in any reasoning from ends, an analyst who says that some action has a function must also name the end for which the action is allegedly functional. No behavior is simply "functional," and any true functional analysis must specify both the system within which the behavior takes place and the end which it satisfies. In ascribing a function to a role in a social system, we

* Werner Stark describes this method of explanation as follows: "Confronted with many phenomena which at first sight appear strange, nay ridiculous — for instance the widespread custom called *couvade* according to which the father must take to his bed while his wife is delivered of the child — [cultural anthropologists] have invariably tried to come to a proper comprehension by seeing the puzzling pieces of behavior as part and parcel of a wider, interlocking system of culture, and asking what possible function the mysterious actions to be explained can conceivably have within the common life. The fundamental idea which guides the effort is clearly the conviction that a social system can meaningfully be described as a unity — a unity within which every element can shed light on every other because they are all organically — or, as it is usually expressed, functionally — related." *The Fundamental Forms of Social Thought* (London: Routledge & Kegan Paul, 1962), p. 76.

mean in every case that it serves either the survival, or the adjustment, or the maintenance of the system. This is the most commonly assumed end in social systems analysis, and it conforms to the empirical generalization that, *ceteris paribus*, societies do persist beyond the life-span of individual members.*

Failure to bear in mind the need to "relativize" statements of functionality has led in the past to various errors which have reflected adversely on the method of functionalism. Some analysts have been so sure that all social activity, bizarre as well as routine, was functional that they have blinded themselves to instances of genuinely disruptive or dysfunctional behavior. The use of functional explanations without specific reference to a system's ends may produce this kind of insidious "normative functionalism," in which the analyst winds up pleading that even patently antisocial behavior or the disruptive consequences of some form of organization must be tolerated because they are functional. However, no action is functional per se, and the analyst must show that a role or an institution is, or is not, functional for the existence and persistence of the system.[12] Although Parsons has been mistaken by some readers for a normative functionalist, he himself has warned against the dangers of not making functions relative to an end: "The most essential condition of successful dynamic analysis is continual and systematic reference of every problem to the state of the system as a whole. . . . Functional significance in this context is inherently teleological. A process or set of conditions either 'contributes' to the maintenance (or development) of the system or it is 'dysfunctional' in

* We may note the conclusions on this point of two leading analysts of functionalism. Dorothy Emmet writes: "But where the purpose is not specified, or where we are reluctant to ascribe deliberate purpose at all, as in the case of biological organisms, the unexpressed presumption is likely to be that the function of an element is to be considered as the way in which it helps the system to persist and maintain itself in some form of recognizable continuity." *Function, Purpose and Powers* (London: Macmillan, 1958), pp. 46–47. Carl Hempel asserts categorically, "It is essential . . . for functional analysis as a scientific procedure that its key concepts be explicitly construed as relative to some standard of survival or adjustment." "The Logic of Functional Analysis," in Llewellyn Gross, ed., *Symposium on Sociological Theory* (New York: Harper & Row, 1959), pp. 295–96.

that it detracts from the integration and effectiveness of the system."[13]

Another kind of error committed by functionalists is their uncritical use of the organic analogy. The biological sciences have long employed and continue to make extensive use of systems theory. For example, physiologists speak of the function of a part, such as the heart, in maintaining the life of a living organism; and the organism is seen as a systematic arrangement of such parts. Using the method of analogy, social scientists have sometimes studied societies as if they too were living organisms. As Alvin Gouldner has observed, however, "The recurrent use of organismic models by leading contributors to functionalism, such as Durkheim and Radcliffe-Brown, has its major intellectual justification in the fact that organisms are *examples* of systems. To the extent that the organismic model has proved fruitful in sociological analysis it has become so because the organism was a paradigmatic case of a system. . . . Indeed, we might say that the organismic model has been misleading in sociological analysis precisely insofar as it led to a focus on characteristics which were peculiar to the organism but not inherent in a generalized notion of a 'system.' "[14]

Examples of such misplaced organic analogies include the belief that social systems have life cycles (birth, adolescence, maturity, old age, and death) and the belief that social systems cannot freely change their structures because individual organisms cannot freely change theirs. Even the belief of the "normative functionalists" that all behavior would be functional if only we understood the entire system is a product of the organic analogy badly conceived. None of these ideas is basic to systems theory; and functionalism, as a method for analyzing how systems operate, is not in any way dependent on the organic analogy for its intellectual rationale.

Having indicated that a social system serves the end of its own persistence, let us try to conceptualize how this end is achieved. What kinds of work must the actors in a social system accomplish in order for their system to survive? Or, to put it another way, what is the minimal content of the roles which are to be differentiated, assigned, and legitimatized in a functional social system? In recent years, social scientists have proposed various lists of "functional prerequisites for a social system," but the problem remains a major research topic on the theoretical frontiers of political science, sociology, and anthropology. Aberle and his colleagues attempted to solve it by conceptualizing four conditions, any one of which if realized would terminate a social system. These four conditions are: (a) the biological extinction or dispersion of the members; (b) the apathy of the members (a condition that appears to be similar to Durkheim's *anomie*);* (c) the war of all against all; and (d) the absorption of the society into another society.

In order to prevent or avoid the realization of any or all of these conditions, according to Aberle, *et al.*, a social system must perform nine functions. It must: (1) make provision for an adequate relation of the system to the environment and for sexual recruitment; (2) differentiate and make assignments to roles; (3) provide facilities for communications, e.g., speech, writing, etc.; (4) provide a basis for "shared cognitive orientations" among its members; (5) articulate and legitimatize the society's goal or goals; (6) regulate normatively the means of interaction in the society (including the resolution of conflicts); (7) regulate affective expressions, e.g., anger, love, lust, etc.; (8) socialize newcomers; and (9) control disruptive forms of behavior, that is, control deviants.[15]

This is a suggestive list, but one that poses certain difficulties. As we pointed out in Chapter Two, "shared cognitive orientations" need not exist in any social system so long as individuals can predict each other's overt behavior. Another difficulty of the Aberle prerequisites is that several of them should be combined and reduced to a single, more fundamental requirement. It is important that functional imperatives be conceived abstractly, for if a list is merely descriptive, it will suggest concrete roles which may be required in one system but not in all systems. We

---

* Sebastian de Grazia writes, with regard to *anomie*, "It stands in contrast to *solidarité*, the expression Durkheim used to designate the perfect integration of a society with clear-cut values that define the status of each member of the community." *The Political Community: A Study of Anomie* (Chicago: University of Chicago Press, 1948), p. 4.

therefore need a more analytical conceptualization of functional prerequisites.

Talcott Parsons has suggested four sets of functional needs which must be met by any social system if it is to exist and persist.[16] The first of these is "pattern maintenance," or socialization. In meeting this need, the system must insure that the values and norms of the system are transmitted to children and immigrants. In the case of children, this is accomplished chiefly by inculcating within their maturing personalities a conscience, or superego, and by training them in the habits of discipline ("deferred gratification") and socially tolerated forms of behavior (e.g., competitive activities) for reducing the personal tensions generated by socialized life. Socialization is carried out chiefly through the institutions of the family and formal education, and through the daily experiencing of societal norms which define conformity.

A second functional need is that of adaptation to the environment, including the differentiation and assignment of roles, the envalued distribution of scarce resources, and the anticipation of environmental changes. The roles and norms of economic activity are devoted to meeting this functional need (e.g., markets, central planning institutions, and technological institutes). Closely related to adaptation is the third functional requirement — "goal attainment." Each actor, group, and subsystem within an integrated social system has one or more goals — e.g., businesses seek to make money, churches to win converts, schools to educate students, mothers to protect their children, armies to win battles, and so forth — and the system as a whole has goals, for example, in relation to other systems.

Obviously, these goals often conflict with each other. Goal attainment involves the processing of particular wills in order to produce a consensus, usually temporary and often artificial, on priorities and policies for achieving goals. Goal attainment also involves the mobilization and allocation of a system's resources as required by its policies. It is political institutions that are explicitly concerned with solving this functional problem, but political types of relationships (i.e., the use of power and influence by some people to manipulate the behavior of others) may exist at all levels of a society as individuals try to reach decisions or achieve a consensus on their particular goals. If a deadlock rather than a consensus develops at the level where decisions are to be enforced by authority, a "power deflation" will ensue.

Parsons's fourth functional prerequisite is that of integration and social control. It is fulfilled positively by roles and institutions that perpetuate, assert, or demonstrate the basic values of the system, on which integration is based — for example, the roles and institutions of statesmen, judicial courts of last resort, religious leaders, artists, creative interpreters of the culture, and even social critics. It is also fulfilled negatively through the exercise of authority to control deviancy, regulate conflict, and adjudicate disputes. The ultimate integrative organ of a social system is the state — i.e., the institutionalized set of roles entrusted with the authoritative exercise of force.

The functional prerequisite of integration is of the greatest interest to the student of revolution. As we have seen, if there were only two functional prerequisites, integration and socialization, then the need for integrative action would decline to the extent that socialization approached perfect efficiency. If values were completely consistent with each other and if they were perfectly transmitted to each member of a system (assuming biological equality), deviancy would disappear. However, a society must not only socialize newcomers into the value structure; it must also adapt to its environment. Adaptation itself generates conflicts of interest, which the integrative institutions must regulate. Equally important, the relationship between the particular values which are socialized into actors and the roles these actors play in adapting to the environment generates varying demands for integrative action. When the socialized values and the requirements of adaptation virtually coincide, integrative tasks will decline to residual problems of deviancy and the authoritative resolution of conflicts of interest. As socialized values and the requirements of adaptation diverge, however, the tasks of integration become proportionately greater.

In these situations, truly creative action by the leaders of a system is required. They must maintain some degree of integration, even if only through the exercise of physical force; at the same time, they must mobilize and inspire innovations in all roles in order to resynchronize the values and environment. They may attempt these tasks by entering the policy-making arena and advancing a positive program of reform, or they may try to achieve some coherence in roles by replacing a system's irreconcilable goals with a single, apocalyptic one, such as the overcoming of a foreign threat. They may also consciously advance a surrogate for the old value structure, such as a claim to "charismatic" authority, and this may later be routinized as a form of stable authority (e.g., the Emperor myth of Meiji Japan). Whatever is attempted, in times of change the integrative institutions become the vital center where threats of revolution will either remain benign or become malignant.

These four categories of functions — socialization, adaptation, goal-attainment, and integration — comprehend the work that a system must do in order to survive. However, the application of these prerequisites to any functioning social system raises questions about what precisely we mean by survival. As Hempel has said: "For the sake of objective testability of functional hypotheses, it is essential . . . that definitions of needs or functional prerequisites be supplemented by reasonably clear and objectively applicable criteria of what is to be considered a healthy state or a normal working order of the systems under consideration; and that the vague and sweeping notion of survival then be construed in the relativized sense of survival in a healthy state as specified."[17]

There are various ways in which social scientists have tried to conceptualize the healthy state of the social system. One of these is through the notion of equilibrium.

According to Emmet, the term " 'Equilibrium' should only be used where it is possible to show that customs [norms], institutions, and the social activities related to them [roles] dovetail in together in certain specified ways so that one provides a corrective to disruptive tendencies in another. It should also be possible to show how, if these functional relationships are lacking, a form of social life will break down; and also to show how a reacting tendency may go too far."[18] Equilibrium as used by Emmet, and as we shall use it here, thus means "homeostatic equilibrium." Homeostasis, a concept borrowed from physiology, refers to the fact that "processes within the body control and counteract variations which would destroy the system if they exceeded more than a limited range."[19] Wallace, in defining the principle of homeostasis as it is used in social systems analysis, has said that it consists of "coordinated actions (including 'cultural' actions [legitimate actions]) by all or some of [a social system's] parts, to preserve its own integrity by maintaining a minimally fluctuating, life-supporting matrix for its individual members, and [that] will, under stress, take emergency measures to preserve the constancy of this matrix."[20]

We have already discussed several of the homeostatic, or matrix-maintaining, processes that take place within a social system — e.g., the control of deviancy, the avoidance and routinization of relations of conflict, coercive actions to maintain integration during a power deflation, normative definitions of social mobility, and many others. We have also mentioned that value sharing endows a social system with a homeostatic capacity. An example of how this works can be found in the rules of competition by which a system brings relationships of conflict under control. As Dahrendorf has observed, "For effective conflict regulation to be possible, both parties to a conflict have to recognize the necessity and reality of the conflict situation and, in this sense, the fundamental justice of the cause of the opponent."[21] The antagonists must, in short, share the same values. Only when they do share values can they agree upon the norms which, in turn, will allow them to pursue their conflict of interest without resorting to violence. Since values are an independent variable, but one that interacts with the concrete requirements of adaptation to the environment, the homeostatic capacity of a system will be determined by value sharing *and* by the potency of these values with respect to a given environment.

Obviously, a homeostatic equilibrium is not a static equilibrium, and to call it a "moving equilibrium," as some social theorists do, is to beg most of the difficult questions. What is meant by a "moving equilibrium"? Although it is rarely defined, a moving equilibrium appears to resemble the physicists' concept of "dynamic equilibrium," in which mass and velocity remain the same, as for example in a spinning top. The concept of homeostatic equilibrium in a social system, however, does not depend upon some notion of a constant social mass moving at a constant velocity. A social system in equilibrium is perfectly capable of absorbing new actors into the system of action and of altering the tempo of interactions in order to meet its functional prerequisites. Homeostatic equilibrium differs from either static or dynamic equilibrium in that it depends solely upon the existence and stability of the various processes for fulfilling the functional prerequisites of a social system and for solving, short of violence, a series of problems that arise and are predictable within a particular cultural gestalt (i.e., within a value-environmental symbiosis).

Can a homeostatic equilibrium change? Among systems theorists, most of whom recognize that societal equilibrium must be homeostatic, there are numerous disagreements over this question. Most theorists would agree in defining change as differences in structural configurations (or what Wilbert Moore calls "coexistences") which have been observed over time. The argument is over whether the concept of a social system maintaining itself through homeostatic processes can accommodate such structural changes. For example, Dahrendorf, who believes that homeostatic processes and structural change are incommensurate, has written: "By change . . . we do not mean the occurrence of certain processes within a given structural pattern, for this is accounted for by the category of structure in any case. Regular processes within objects that have a structure — such as the processes of role allocation, or of socialization of new members of society — are indeed an essential element of every structure. Structural analysis is essentially the analysis of such processes [i.e., homeostatic processes]. What is meant [by change] is, rather, that the entire structural arrangement of so-called forms of society can change."[22]

In contrast to this view of Dahrendorf's, the position taken here is that homeostatic equilibrium is fully compatible with one form (although not with all forms) of observed structural change. As we have already seen, role requirements consist of ranges of tolerable behavior. Innovations occurring within these ranges may in time lead to slight modifications of the ranges themselves. Similarly, personal differences and slight variations in socialization over a period of time will give rise to sequences of small changes that taken together may result in partial or total changes of structure.

Processes of growth or differentiation (increased functional specificity of roles) are changes of this sort, and they may ultimately produce an entirely different social structure.

These kinds of changes in systems may occur without disturbing a homeostatic equilibrium so long as the value structure and the environment *change in synchronization with each other*. An environmental change, such as the introduction of agriculture into a hunting and gathering economy, need not destroy the society's equilibrium so long as the value structure alters to accommodate the gradually changing division of labor. On the other hand, it is perfectly possible that the old value structure cannot accommodate such a change. In many hunting and gathering societies, for example, it is considered the women's role to collect vegetables. If agriculture is introduced so rapidly that men cannot reevaluate their own roles in terms of agricultural labor, equilibrium will be destroyed. But there is nothing in the concept of homeostatic equilibrium to suggest that such changes must automatically destroy the equilibrium. A more recent example of gradual structural change within the context of homeostatic equilibrium is that associated with the integration of white immigrant communities into the United States' division of labor during the past century.

The equilibrium of a social system depends upon the degree of synchronization between its values and its division of labor. Since these two variables also determine a system's structure, as they change, social structure will change. Dahrendorf's belief that routine social processes (which taken together create a homeostatic equilibrium) are somehow different from structural changes derives in part from a misapplication of the organic analogy. It is true that an organism cannot change the structure of its organs (e.g., its liver, heart, stomach). However, while a healthy organism is a system in homeostatic equilibrium, not every system in homeostatic equilibrium is an organism. A social system can change its structure and still remain equilibrated.*

---

* Just as homeostatic equilibrium is compatible with a form of structural change, it is also compatible with structural changes initiated from within a system. Those critics of structural-functionalism who contend that equilibrium rules out all but external sources of change are looking at the structural-functional model only in its pure value theory formulation,

A different and more important criticism of the equilibrium model is that homeostatic equilibrium is incompatible with purposeful change of a social structure. This point is valid, but it does not destroy the usefulness of the equilibrium model; it merely expands the category of social change. So far we have argued that homeostatic social processes often result in small, incremental changes which, over time, may amount to a change of structure. Nevertheless, the actors who make these adjustments have no intention of bringing about a structural change in the system. They are merely concerned with mild reforms, such as resolving a dispute, or rewarding a novel performance of a familiar role, or removing an inconsistency in a norm (e.g., a mediator awards higher wages to workers in a labor dispute, or an educator decides to replace textbooks with televised lectures).

A very different kind of change occurs when actors recognize that an internal innovation, or an external threat, or some other pressure, is destroying the system's equilibrium and that structural change is necessary if the society is to survive. In these cases, the concern of the actor, as well as of the analyst, is not with homeostatic processes but with conscious policies and the processes of policy formation (e.g., the purposes of American leaders in issuing the Emancipation Proclamation to end slavery). Structure-changing *policies* are needed precisely because some sudden or unfamiliar situation has exceeded the capacities of customary homeostatic practices. It is only in these kinds of situations that the threat of revolution exists, and the analyst of revolution must be concerned with both the determinants of the situation which demands structural change and the *purposive* responses to it.

To make a revolution is to accept violence for the purpose of causing the system to change; more exactly, it is the purposive implementation of a strategy of violence in order to effect a change in social structure. Revolution also develops in part because some

---

which we have modified. For examples of the opinion that equilibrium is inconsistent with endogenous change, see Wilbert Moore, "A Reconsideration of Theories of Social Change," *American Sociological Review,* XXV (December 1960), 811; and Ralf Dahrendorf, "Out of Utopia," *The American Journal of Sociology,* LXIV (September 1958), 121. The exogenous/endogenous distinction is taken up in detail in the next chapter.

people have purposes contrary to those of the revolutionaries regarding the desirability, amount, and direction of change. However, these cross-purposes *concerning structural change* do not arise in a system which enjoys homeostatic equilibrium. They arise only in the dysfunctional social system, the one whose values do not synchronize with its division of labor.

The distinction between changes undertaken routinely to maintain an equilibrium and changes undertaken in order to recreate an equilibrium provides the key to a basic typology of social changes. The basis of the typology is the factor of purposive change of social structure. One kind of change, the only kind that is compatible with homeostatic equilibrium, is "evolutionary" change. Such evolutionary changes are made by actors in systems, but the intentions of the actors in making them are not to bring about structural changes, evolutionary or otherwise. If structural change occurs under these circumstances, it is an *unintended consequence* of actions which are undertaken for different purposes.   Unintentional, evolutionary changes thus constitute one class of structural changes, and they are the only class that may occur without disturbing the equilibrium of a system.

The other main class of changes includes the results of conscious policies of structural change pursued by actors within the system (including what may be unintended results produced by a purposeful policy of structural change). This second class of changes can be subdivided into two types: (1) "conservative" change, which serves two ends: structural change and the avoidance of violence; and (2) "insurrectionary" change, which serves only the end of change itself. Both of these types of change occur only in the already disequilibrated social system, and they occur chiefly as a consequence of the system's being in disequilibrium. However, the occurrence and the quality of conservative change directly influence the likelihood of whether insurrectionary change will ever occur at all.

4

The disequilibrated
social system

ERIC HOFFER has observed, "We are usually told
that revolutions are set in motion to realize radical changes. Actually, it is drastic change which sets the stage for revolution. The
revolutionary mood and temper are generated by the irritations,
difficulties, hungers, and frustrations inherent in the realization of
drastic change. Where things have not changed at all, there is the
least likelihood of revolution."[1] After surveying military revolutions from ancient times to the twentieth century, T. H. Wintringham reached a similar conclusion: "The puzzle becomes not
why did the mutiny occur, but why did men, for years or generations, endure the torments against which in the end they revolted."[2] The point of both of these comments is that people in
societies are not inherently mutinous. Society is a form of human
interaction that transcends violence, of which one form is revolution. Revolutions are in this sense antisocial, testifying to the existence of extraordinary dissatisfactions among people with a
particular form of society. They do not occur randomly, and they
need not occur at all. Revolution can be rationally contemplated

only in a society that is undergoing radical structural change and that is in need of still further change.

Many societies have undertaken radical changes very rapidly without experiencing revolution (e.g., the United States during the Great Depression). An analysis of the causes and the configurations of a changing society, therefore, cannot provide a complete explanation of the occurrence of revolution. But such an analysis is the inescapable first step on the way toward explaining a revolution; a changing society is a necessary but not a sufficient cause of any revolution, and political violence that occurs in an equilibrated society, although it may be called "revolutionary," requires a different but related form of analysis (e.g., the analysis of subversion, non-revolutionary coups d'état, palace "revolutions," and so forth). In order to portray the changing society, we must explore the disequilibrated social system in both its systemic (macroscopic) and personal (microscopic) dimensions. The previous discussion of the functional social system provides us with the tools and criteria for describing the disequilibrated social system — the stage upon which revolutionary action takes place.

So long as a society's values and the realities with which it must deal in order to exist are in harmony with each other, the society is immune from revolution. When a society is in homeostatic equilibrium, it is continuously receiving stimuli from its members and from the outside that cause it to make adjustments in its division of labor and its structure of values. It may go on receiving these stimuli (e.g., innovations, new tastes, cultural borrowings, etc.) and making the necessary changes indefinitely, without experiencing revolution, so long as it keeps its values and its environment in synchronization. Change of this sort is evolutionary and does not directly interest us here.

On certain occasions, however, social systems which were previously functioning in equilibrium move out of equilibrium. These situations pose a threat, not necessarily immediate but still a threat, to the continuation of the system. Purposeful changes must be undertaken in order to recreate a homeostatic equilibrium, and if a new equilibrium is reached it will usually differ from the one that was destroyed. Before considering these policies of change and how they may succeed or fail, let us look at some of the forces that cause a functional society to lose its equilibrium, thereby generating a demand for policies of change.

For many years social scientists have been compiling lists of influences or occurrences that appear to have been the causes of revolutionary situations. In 1944, Gottschalk suggested the following list of what are actually both causes and effects of revolutions: "land hunger, taxation, high fees for services rendered and for services not rendered, exclusion from certain kinds of prestige or from certain kinds of office, misgovernment, bad roads, commercial restrictions, corruption, military or diplomatic defeat, famine, high prices, low wages, and unemployment."[3] Without in the least questioning that all these phenomena have, at various times and in various societies, promoted revolutionary conditions, we must conclude that this list is useless. For one thing, it is in no way oriented toward relative standards (e.g., how a people may have envisaged good roads), which would allow us to infer that a change in either values or environment had occurred.

Anthony Wallace approaches the problem somewhat more analytically. "The severe disorganization of a socio-cultural system," he writes, "may be caused by the impact of any one or combination of a variety of forces which push the system beyond the limits of equilibrium. Some of these forces are: climatic or faunal changes which destroy the economic basis of its existence; epidemic disease which grossly alters the population structure; wars which exhaust the society's resources of manpower or result in defeat or invasion; internal conflict among interest groups which results in extreme disadvantage for at least one group; and, very commonly, a position of perceived subordination and inferiority with respect to an adjacent society."[4] This list is more valuable than Gottschalk's since it relates certain forces that can disrupt either the values or the division of labor, or both, to a social system's equilibrium. Nevertheless, Wallace's list can only be regarded as suggestive. It makes no distinction between forces that impinge upon the values and those that affect the environment, and it offers no clue as to why the disruption of values or the environment produces disequilibrium.

A much older and entirely different conception of the changing society derives from Alexis de Tocqueville's classic study of the French Revolution. It used to be known as the "feudal reaction" theory, but in its present-day form, it is more commonly called "the 'revolution' of rising expectations." Among the numerous discoveries that Tocqueville made in his social history of the eighteenth century was the fact that the people of France were enjoying relative prosperity on the eve of the 1789 revolution. In a passage that has been repeatedly quoted (e.g., by Hoffer[5] and by Gerschenkron[6]), Tocqueville observed: "It was precisely in those parts of France where there had been most improvement that popular discontent ran highest. This may seem illogical — but history is full of such paradoxes. For it is not always when things are going from bad to worse that revolution breaks out. On the contrary, it oftener happens that when a people which has put up with an oppressive rule over a long period without protest suddenly finds the government relaxing its pressure, it takes up arms against it."[7]

Tocqueville argued that real economic conditions were slightly improved just prior to the revolution, but that the nobility, already weakened by the growth of economic power in the third estate and undercut by an increasingly ineffective central government, thrust itself into this expanding economy in an effort to recapture some of its medieval privileges. This "feudal reaction" allegedly caused the revolution. It is very important to understand that Tocqueville did not rest his case on this single line of analysis; he also gave great weight to popular dissatisfaction with the clergy, to the influence of powerful revolutionary ideologues, and to monarchical practices that the people resented as much as they did the privileges of the nobility. Moreover, his idea of a "feudal reaction" is more an analysis of the final causes of insurrection than it refers to the remote causes of a changing society.

Nevertheless, some students of revolution have seized on Tocqueville's idea of frustrated expectations in a period of improving economic conditions to generalize about the causes of revolution. Although there are several exponents of this view, James Davies is representative. "Revolutions," he writes, "are most likely to occur when a prolonged period of objective economic and social development is followed by a short period of sharp reversal. . . . The crucial factor is the vague or specific fear that ground gained over a long period of time will be quickly lost." And: "The background for political instability is economic and social progress. A populace in a static socio-economic condition is very unlikely to listen to the trumpet or siren call to rebellion. . . . Progress in other words is most of the time a necessary but insufficient cause for violent political change."[8]

While there is no doubt that socioeconomic *change* lies behind any revolution, is this change of a "progressive" sort? We doubt that it is (no noticeable progress led to the Indian Mutiny, 1857–59; the Irish Rebellion, 1916–23; the Spanish Civil War, 1936–39; the Chinese Revolution, 1947–49; or the Cuban Revolution, 1959), and even if it were, we doubt that progress can be meaningfully conceptualized. Change in a system whose values and environment are in synchronization can be either progressive or regressive without a revolution occurring; but if its values and environment are dissynchronized, regardless of the direction in which the one or the other has moved, a threat of revolution always exists. The theory of "rising expectations" contributes something to this basic analytical proposition, but it is overgeneralized and cannot be made relative to standards of neutral or declining expectations.

Another challenge to the theory of rising expectations is its direct opposite — namely, the view that revolutions are caused by extreme inequities in the distribution of income. Whereas some theorists see economic growth as a precondition of revolution, others believe that economic decline and its effects, unequally shared in the system, lead to revolution. Representative of this view is Alfred Meusel's contribution to the *Encyclopedia of the Social Sciences:* "The quality of the change characterized as revolution cannot be grasped without consideration of the type of society in which it occurs. This may be described in highly simplified terms as a society torn by an internal antagonism between a small upper class which by virtue of its proprietary claims to certain sources of income receives a considerable portion of the social product and a large lower class which performs all the manual, routine labor and subsists in relative poverty."[9]

One obvious drawback of this analysis is that some of the most stable societies on earth have been characterized by extreme differentials of income among social strata. In China, for example, no antagonisms existed among these strata for centuries-long periods. Antagonisms did develop on certain occasions, but Meusel's description offers us neither an understanding of why this happened nor a basis for distinguishing between conditions of inequality without antagonism and conditions of inequality with antagonism. On the basis of his hypothesis we should expect to find that Negro slaves in America or Hindu outcastes in India were historically the most rebellious social groups. Actually we know that both of these groups were among the least rebellious so long as their values and their environment synchronized with each other. Neither can the American Civil War nor the Satsuma Rebellion in Japan (1877) be understood simply as a war of the poor against the rich. Barnett's conclusion on the effects of depriving people of "essential" material products is inescapable: " 'Deprivation' . . . refers to the elimination of something that a person believes he has the right to expect. . . . 'Essentials' is an entirely relative term. It takes on meaning only in the light of the system of values of a specific ethnic group."[10]

A much more promising approach to this problem is to construct an analytical typology which recognizes that the primary determinant of a social system's equilibrium is the degree of value-environmental synchronization. Wilbert Moore suggested this method by breaking down sources of change into two categories: "(1) the ubiquity of the 'environmental challenge,' and (2) the ubiquity of non-conformity and of failure to achieve ideal values."[11] Although we must reorient Moore's second category somewhat to stress the functions of values in providing a symbolic interpretation of reality, these two categories, combined with a further distinction between exogenous (externally derived) and endogenous (arising within the system) sources of change, can provide us with a theoretically meaningful typology of the pressures which may destroy a system's equilibrium. We shall refer to such pressures as "sources of change" and study the effects of each under one of four headings: (1) exogenous value-changing sources; (2) endogenous value-changing sources; (3) exogenous environment-changing sources; and (4) endogenous environment-changing sources. After examining each category separately, we shall then investigate why, together or individually, they sometimes swamp the homeostatic capacities of a social system.

Exogenous sources of value change are very familiar. Global communications; the rise of external "reference groups" (e.g., the effects of the French and Russian revolutions on neighboring populations, or the effects of Negro African republics on the values of colored populations everywhere); the internal mobilizations and refugee migrations caused by wars; and the work of groups such as Christian missionaries, communist parties, the Peace Corps, and UNESCO – all have led to culture contact and to the invidious comparisons this generates. It is of course true that the effects of culture contact in dissolving particular value structures have usually been reinforced by exogenous sources of environmental change (notably by colonialism). Without environment-changing sources to "open" a society to external influences, a functional domestic value structure would be likely to cause a population to reject foreign values, much as Frenchmen in Pascal's day believed in the existence of "vérité en deçà des Pyrénées, erreur au delà."[12] Even so, exogenous sources of value change should be distinguished analytically, and sought in the context of narrow time spans or individual lives, they are readily isolable. For example, the effect of foreign education and travel on many students from European colonies was primarily to alter their values.

Endogenous sources of value change are equally familiar, but they are considerably harder to conceptualize. They include, for example, the displacement of religious authorities by secular monarchs in both the early modern Christian and Islamic worlds; Henry VIII's impact on the value structure of England while he was trying to resolve his marital difficulties; the corrosive effects of the theories of Bacon, Descartes, and others, on Scholasticism; and, generally speaking, changes in values that are brought about as a result of intellectual developments and the acceptance of creative innovations. These changes are hard to conceptualize because values, by their very nature, are resistant to changes other than "homeostatic interpretations." Being the definitional and explanatory symbols of a system, values claim universality and exclusive jurisdiction within that system. They have the power to brand alternatives as deviant "heresies" or mental aberrations, and defenders of a value structure frequently exercise this power.

Endogenous sources of value change consist primarily of internal "innovations" which affect the value structure much as technological innovations (e.g., the invention of the cotton gin) affect adaptation to the environment. In fact, care must be taken not to confuse these two sources of endogenous change. By endogenous sources of value change we mean those innovations that impinge directly on a value structure, and not those that influence values secondarily, as a result of changes in the environment. When the environment changes, for whatever reason, it becomes dissynchronized with the value structure, encouraging men to formulate expressions of value which lead to changes in the value structure and which resynchronize values with the pattern of environmental adaptation. These resynchronizing changes may be produced homeostatically, or by purposeful nonviolent processes, or by revolution. But when the actual source of change in a system impinges initially on the environment, it should be classified as either exogenous or endogenous environmental change. This point is equally valid in reverse. Initial changes of values, for whatever reason (e.g., the conversion of a people to Catholicism) will produce reverberatory changes in the division of labor (e.g., larger families, more celebate men and women, and church attendance on Sunday and other religious occasions).

There have always been two main problems in studying either value or technological innovation: how to account for creative, or innovative, behavior itself, and how to account for the acceptance or rejection by a system of the products of innovation. These questions continue to be the subjects of philosophical, psychological, and social science research; and at present there is only a modicum of agreement on answers to them. With regard to the origins of innovative behavior, most scholarship has concentrated on the determinants of the innovator's personality, or on answering the question: "Who are the innovators?" There are several theories, probably the most famous being Erik Erikson's, here summarized by Everett Hagen. "A reformer," Hagen writes, "is an individual who learned when a child a pattern of solution of a personal problem that caused him intense anxiety. . . . When the individual faced in adult life a social force . . . parallel to the deeply troublesome force of his childhood, his anxiety was rearoused and he reacted as he had learned to react in childhood. If the evil discerned by an individual who has thus been sensitized in his childhood is also perceived by enough fellow members of his society as an evil, they will follow his lead and he may accomplish a great social change and become an historic figure for good or evil."[13] In his well-known book, *Young Man Luther*, Erikson applied this theory to analyze the value innovations made by Martin Luther.

In addition to Erikson's analysis, there are several other positive theories of innovation, including those that postulate human instincts to play, to explore, to "satisfy curiosity," and so forth.[14] In this present context, we need only assume that human beings do possess an unevenly distributed capacity to innovate — that is, to alter or recombine what Barnett calls "mental configurations."[15] The more serious problem then becomes what happens to the products of innovation. Why are they sometimes accepted, and why are they more usually rejected?

Social systems normally control the influence of innovations by attracting them into certain fields through the offer of rewards to innovators. This has the effect of "routinizing" innovation. As Barnett points out, "Innovation flourishes in an atmosphere of anticipation of it."[16] Thus, in Western culture we reward the "creative" arts and distinguish between a creative composer and a re-creative performer (who may nevertheless make small changes in his role). In recent decades, a process of rewarding and anticipating innovations in the physical and biological sciences has developed because such innovations have been found to serve market and defense functions in the contemporary nation-state type of social system.

Only occasionally is an innovation produced or accepted in an unexpected sphere, such as the value structure. There are two alternative but complementary schools of opinion that attempt to explain this occurrence.[17] One is the "marginal man" or "cultural hybrid" hypothesis, according to which persons who occupy new, or poorly defined, or ambiguous statuses (such as those associated with being a Negro *and* a physician or a longshoreman *and* a philosopher in America) are likely to be innovators or receptive to innovations. It is argued that such a person has a need to reduce personal tensions and that his ambiguous status affords him a rather emancipated view of the social structure and its stereotypes. Cultural hybrids (e.g., the Jew emerging from the Ghetto) may be produced through homeostatic processes (e.g., social mobility, or co-option into an elite) or as a result of historical "accidents" such as adoption, being orphaned, and so forth. When an innovator belongs to a marginal group, his innovations may be accepted throughout the group. The group may then present a challenge to the value structure, and this confrontation may cause a competition over values to develop. More commonly, if the innovative values of the marginal group are attractive to the general society, they will be incorporated and legitimatized within the overall value structure, producing a value change (e.g., the absorption of some Taoist perspectives into the predominantly Confucian values of traditional China).

The complement to the "marginal man" hypothesis is that of the high-status, or "prestige-laden," innovator. Often a person with creative abilities in Erikson's sense will occupy a status in society that already commands respect regardless of its occupant. He may then implement his innovations simply by exercising his influence. Alternatively, the occupant of an authority status may carry out an innovation even though this may produce a power deflation and demand the use of physical force to maintain integration. In both cases the mechanism which causes an innovation to be adopted is the tendency of lower-status occupants to respect and imitate the behavior of prestige-laden or "opinion-leading" individuals. Examples include the value changes made by reform-minded monarchs, Japanese samurai of the nineteenth century, some Popes, "modernizing oligarchs" in some Afro-Asian countries today,[18] and so forth. The prestige-laden individual need not, of course, possess creative talents himself in order to bring about change. Conflicts within a value structure resulting from independent lines of intellectual inquiry (e.g., scientific challenges to religious values) have often been resolved in favor of change when an innovator gained the ear of a monarch. Whether or not the changed values can then be synchronized successfully with the environment depends on other circumstances.[19]

Marginal men or innovating elites may, of course, arise as a result of exogenous sources of change (e.g., through the processes of "social mobilization" described by Karl Deutsch).[20] However, successful innovators may also develop within a system and make their influence felt through the system's normal homeostatic processes. It is a naïve or overly formal model of the social system which demands that they arise solely as a result of external influences.

Innovative ability is a trait of human nature that is never allowed full rein in a society but that can never be entirely suppressed. As Eric Hoffer has written, "To make of human affairs a coherent, precise, predictable whole one must ignore or suppress man as he really is, and treat human nature as a mere aspect of nature. The theoreticians do it by limiting the shaping forces of man's destiny to nonhuman factors: providence, the cosmic spirit, geography, climate, economic or physiochemical factors. The practical men of power try to eliminate the human variable by inculcating iron discipline or blind faith, by dissolving the unpredictable individual in a compact group, by subjecting the individual's judgment and will to a ceaseless barrage of propaganda, and by sheer coercion."[21] Unfortunately, the successful transcendence of a state of nature and the prosperity generated by a division of labor depend upon the very routinization Hoffer deplores. It is all the more surprising that some people do occasionally throw off the harness and, despite the mechanisms of social control, make innovations. Even more unusual, such innovations are occasionally influential.

The need for study of innovation and its acceptance applies to sources of environmental change as well as to sources of value change. Exogenous influences on the pattern of adaptation to the environment are obvious. They include the introduction of modern medical knowledge into underdeveloped countries, which often rapidly alters birth and mortality rates; market stimulation as a result of foreign trade; imported technologies and skills; the migrations of populations; and intersystemic diplomatic relations. One particularly important exogenous source of change is military conquest, which introduces new actors, who automatically fill the statuses of authority, into a division of labor. Much time is required for new values to develop which will synchronize with this new division of labor, and until they do develop a permanent "power deflation" exists (e.g., as in Hungary between 1945 and 1956). Sources of endogenous environmental change refer to internal technological innovations, such as the invention of the wheel or the railroad; and an analysis of the origins and acceptance of such innovations is identical with that already made with respect to values. Like innovations in values, technical innovations may be ignored, accepted as toys (as was gunpowder in China), or incorporated into the division of labor, in which case they will produce environmental change and a reverberatory effect on values.

The present fourfold typology — endogenous and exogenous value-changing forces, and endogenous and exogenous environment-changing forces — is one theoretically consistent way to analyze the causes of disequilibrium in a social system. The typology organizes the diverse pressures on a system according to where they originate and what they do. According to this formulation, pressures originate either in the operations of a social system itself or through culture contact, and their influence depends on their effects on the two main determinants of a system's equilibrium: its values and its environment. This is not to say that in a concrete case of social change a particular change-inducing pressure cannot belong to more than one category (e.g., colonialism affects both values and environment), or that more than one change-inducing pressure cannot impinge on the system at any given time. The typology should aid analysis, not inhibit it. For example, a single cause of change, such as imperialism, may have to be broken down into several causes — e.g., into the pressures of foreign merchants and the pressures of foreign missionaries; and in order to determine the precise role of an innovator's actions within a system, the analyst will need both biographical and historical information. Should Peter the Great be considered an innovator and an endogenous source of change within Russia; or should we view the impact of Western ideas and methods on his thinking as exogenous sources of change which were felt in Russia largely through his mediating efforts? Obviously, he cannot be fitted neatly into either category, but the typology at least provides the conceptual tools required for isolating the exogenous and endogenous proportions of his overall contributions to change.

When sources of change do impinge on a social system, one of two circumstances will result: either homeostatic changes will maintain the equilibrium of the system as the pressure is sustained, or the pressure will exceed the homeostatic capacity of the system, producing value-environmental dissynchronization and system disequilibrium. The cause of the second condition is the failure of homeostasis — that is to say, the pressure has been so sudden or so intense or so unprecedented that it has incapacitated the routine institutional procedures and arrangements of a system for self-maintenance. It is then up to the vested leadership of a system to develop policies which will result in resynchronization; for example, changed values may demand a revised arrangement for land distribution, or changed environmental conditions may require that greater political powers be granted to organized labor. As we shall see in the next chapter, whether resynchronization or revolution occurs depends, *ceteris paribus*, on the abilities of these leaders, including their ability to perceive that the system is disequilibrated. Until they act, however, and during the period in which their policies are being implemented, the system will labor under varying degrees of disequilibrium.

A brief example will illustrate some of the uses of our fourfold typology and its relationship to social systems analysis. A popular belief of many Americans is that the causes of the Negro protest movement in the United States after 1954 were primarily a lack of constitutionally-provided civil rights and the systematic segregation of Negroes, as a race, from the rest of the community. Actually these factors have become salient as a result of certain policies that the system's leaders have been attempting to implement in order to resynchronize the system on a new basis. If we can accept the opinions of many Negro observers (for example, Richard Wright and James Baldwin) on Negro conditions, the tragedy of the American race situation was that both Negroes and whites accepted a stable, envalued definition of Negro inferiority — and consequent role assignments — for most of the century after the Civil War. Because Negroes accepted the value structure's explanation of their status, the main body of the Negro population did not support innovations developed by marginal men from their own group, and the resulting relative stability of the system reinforced the stereotypes held by whites, including both those whites who exploited the Negroes and those whose roles did not directly involve Negro labor.

The sources of change which destroyed this equilibrium were

primarily ones that affected Negro values. These sources included the mobilizing experiences of Negro soldiers and domestic migrants during World War II, the rise of reference groups in the form of socially mobile Negroes in America and of Negro African republics with representatives in the United Nations, basic changes in the division of labor of the southeastern states which produced reverberatory changes in values, and several others. The effect of these sources of change was to mobilize a large, chiefly urban Negro population which came to have values roughly identical with those existing in the general society. Given these values, the Negro could no longer continue to accept assignments to roles in the division of labor which were not based on general achievement criteria. Similarly, he had to protest, as any normally socialized American would have, those processes which worked to exclude him from political participation, economic markets, and equal educational opportunities. These processes no longer cohered with his value structure, and they thereby became illegitimate.

This situation could not be repaired homeostatically — court decisions were not routinely obeyed in many states, and new segregation laws in the South, as well as laws to defend white property elsewhere, could not recreate the old equilibrium — so that the system became dysfunctional in several of its processes (e.g., a threat to the power of the Supreme Court developed). The potentiality of revolution arose in many sectors (viz., the Black Muslims), but was forestalled, as of the time of writing this book, by purposeful policies of reform intended to bring the Negro's position in the division of labor into line with the values newly acquired by many Negroes and by the voting majority of the white population. These policies included new legal norms ending segregation, guarantees of political rights, educational reform intended to provide the Negro with the skills required by the roles that he now feels are attainable, urban rebuilding, and so forth. Without the change in Negro values — which led to a change of a different order in white values — these policies would not have been functional and would not have been undertaken (as they demonstrably were not in the century after the Civil War).[22]

The single, most generalized characteristic of the disequilibrated system is that values no longer provide an acceptable symbolic definition and explanation of existence. This condition has been experienced and described intuitively by many writers over the centuries, one of the most famous descriptions being John Donne's seventeenth-century lament:

> And new philosophy calls all in doubt,
> The element of fire is quite put out;
> The sun is lost, and th'earth, and no man's wit
> Can well direct him where to look for it.
> And freely men confess that this world's spent,
> When in the planets and the firmament
> They seek so many new; they see that this
> Is crumbled out again to his atomies.
> 'Tis all in pieces, all coherence gone.

The analytical problem presented by Donne's poem is to know how many of his contemporaries felt the way he did and to know what some of them did about it. As Pettee has phrased it, "Given that cramp exists, that is, that institutions are out of adjustment to life in a given society, individual purposes feel maladjusted. The consciousness of maladjustment creates an individual tension which leads the maladjusted individual to ponder his situation. Given his imaginative and intellectual powers, this may result in anything from getting drunk to writing a book."[23]

The idea of personal "internal tension" opens up an entirely new range of problems for social systems analysis and for the analysis of revolution because the individual human being constitutes a system that is not identical with the social system. A person's actions in conformity to his roles are parts of the social system and he is, to that extent, involved in the social system; however, an elaboration of the structural configuration and the functional requisites of a system of social action does not exhaust the attributes of the personality system. The two systems are related and mutually influencing, but they are not identical. Our earlier discussion of the organization of motivational diversity and the concept of role in social organization was based upon this inescapable conclusion.

What do we mean by the personality system? We mean the structure of perceptions and images held by a single individual and

created by the interaction of his organic system with the processes
of the social system (i.e., such processes as socialization, role assignment, social control, etc.). Personality is what Wallace has
called the "mazeway," or the "perceptions of both the maze of
physical objects of the environment (internal and external, human
and nonhuman) and also of the ways in which this maze can be
manipulated by the self and others in order to minimize stress. The
mazeway is nature, society, culture, personality, and body image,
as seen by one person."[24] According to Wallace, "The intersec-
tion of a cultural [social] and non-cultural [biologic, e.g., libidi-
nous] system, within an individual locus, inevitably generates a
third system: the personality system of the individual,"[25] and it is
the business of personality psychology to describe the process
whereby this personality system, or mazeway, is created.

Wallace's "mazeway" is an attempt to conceptualize a phenomenon described many years ago by Durkheim: "Because beliefs and
social practices . . . come to us from without, it does not follow
that we receive them passively or without modification. In reflecting on collective institutions and assimilating them for ourselves,
we individualize them and impart to them more or less personal
characteristics. . . . It is for this reason that each one of us creates, in a measure, his own morality, religion, and mode of life.
There is no conformity to social convention that does not com-
prise an entire range of individual shades."[26] The personality
system is thus connected with the social system, but it is never a
one-to-one reflection of it. An individual actor, having made some
reconciliation between his personal needs and social interaction,
may nevertheless appear deviant or insane from the perspective of
the social system, while the social system's values are perfectly
synchronized with its division of labor.

As Durkheim has argued, the personalities of the actors in a social system vary over a wide range, but this range is not infinite,
and the distance between its outer limits is determined by the
functional requisites of the system. In a functional system, the
outer limits of personality variability are set chiefly by means of
the value structure's definitions of "crime" and "sickness." As
Parsons has observed, "Defining an act as a crime, *so long as that
definition is accepted in the community,* is an effective way of

discouraging other people from following that example."[27] In his study of the motives of embezzlers, Cressey comes to a similar conclusion: "The *words* that the potential embezzler uses in his conversations with himself are actually the most important elements in the process which gets him into trouble, or keeps him out of trouble. If he sees a possibility for embezzlement, it is because he has defined the relationship between [his] unshareable problem and an illegal solution in language that lets him look on trust violation as something other than trust violation [e.g., 'borrowing,' 'business is business,' etc.]. If he cannot do this, he does not become an embezzler."[28]

Similarly, with regard to the other main category for classifying deviant behavior — physical or mental illness — Parsons has written: "[Sickness] is, in a certain sense, a functional equivalent of crime, of revolutionary movements, of escapism in the form of some kinds of religious cultism, and so on. . . . In therapy the combination of the sick role and the therapeutic role as part of the social structure constitutes a complex, intricate mechanism of defense against deviance so that deviance that occurs can be channeled into relatively harmless channels. The sick person is isolated from others. It is a very important point that sick people are a category and not a movement. From the point of view of the stability of the social system this is very important indeed."[29]

When the system is disequilibrated, however, the envalued definitions of crime and sickness — that is, the outer limits on personality variability — are relaxed, and this relaxation presents a serious analytical problem for the student of revolution. In a stable system acts of deviancy committed by actors whose particular mazeways lie beyond the limits of toleration established by the system will be identified as criminals or lunatics, even though they themselves may label their acts as "revolutionary." But in the disequilibrated system, some degree of personal tension will be experienced by every actor, possibly leading him to relieve it through behavior that he would have considered deviant before the system lost its equilibrium. Moreover, at these times it becomes increasingly more difficult for other actors in a system to differentiate between behavior that represents a dysfunction-inspired protest and behavior that represents the now-disguised deviancy of a formerly eccentric personality. In a disequilibrated situation, some people will engage in antisocial action because of dysfunction-induced tensions and others will participate because their personalities embody a socially intolerable resolution of biologic and cultural demands. The latter group would have been considered deviants in the equilibrated system, and they will again be controlled as deviants after equilibrium is restored by revolution or otherwise.

The problem is further complicated by the fact that disequilibrated conditions do not normally give rise at once to marked changes in behavior. The behavior of socialized, non-deviant actors will change only slowly and erratically in response to disequilibrium. Since personality and the social system are related, as one changes, so the other must change — but not necessarily at the same rate. This is why a disequilibrated system may persist for some length of time without undergoing immediate disintegration or revolution, and also why the leaders of a social system often fail to perceive the seriousness of a disequilibrated situation until the forces of revolution are well organized. On this point, Herbert Phillips has argued for ". . . the necessity of recognizing theoretically the capacity of individuals in non-congruent situations to bear considerable psychological strain, and still function effectively, maintaining both their prevailing personality patterns and established social structure. . . . Because of the human capacity to resolve psychological strain *internally*, by the use of well-established unconscious psychological defense mechanisms such as repression, denial, etc., much of the behavioral change that we often expect to follow conditions of non-congruence may in fact not occur."[30]

Failure to take into account the systemic inputs into mazeway formation and the system's role in defining deviancy has led in the past to the fallacy of psychological reductionism, particularly in studies of revolutionary behavior.[31] A psychologically reductionist argument ignores the notion that personality is a "third system" and tends to explain all action in terms of Freudian-derived concepts of personal motivation. One particularly heady example is quoted by Harold Lasswell in his *Psychopathology and Politics:* " 'Distrust of father was the chief cause of the [1927] Vienna riot,' said Paul Federn, onetime president of the Psychoanalytical

Society. From a psychoanalytical standpoint all authority is the father, and this formerly for Austria was incorporated in the imposing figure of Emperor Franz Josef. But during the war the father deceived and maltreated his children, and only the material preoccupations of life and the joyous outburst when at the close of the war the old authority broke asunder prevented Austria from having a revolution then. . . . Once the police fired, blood flowed and the mob reacted savagely, responding to the ancient fear of castration by the father which is present in all of us unconsciously in the face of the punishing authority. . . . The Vienna riots were in the deepest sense a family row."[32]

Psychological reductionism refuses to distinguish between acts of political violence that are in response to the needs of an abnormal personality (as defined by a particular equilibrated social system) and acts of political violence that are in response to personal tensions generated in adults by a disequilibrated social system. Instead, psychologically reductionist theories tend to explain all political violence in terms of the displacement of private, probably childhood-derived, neurotic needs onto public objects. Psychological reductionism is particularly dangerous in the analysis of, and in practical attempts to routinize, social conflict within or between functional systems. Many social psychologists have tried to explain all conflict, notably international war, in terms of the need for the release of tensions generated by psychosexual maturation. This is undoubtedly an oversimplification. Just as an individual personality cannot be derived entirely from the social system in which it is formed, the social system and its needs and processes cannot be derived entirely from a study of the personalities that exist within it. Functional social systems depend upon the avoidance and routinization of realistic conflicts among persons whose personalities are within the range of acceptable variation, while at the same time they regulate conflicts which serve the needs of malformed personalities through envalued definitions of crime and insanity and through processes of social control which isolate criminals and lunatics.

Psychological data must be used in the study of revolutionary situations because heightened personal tensions are one certain indicator of systemic disequilibrium, and the personalities of revolutionaries and legitimate authorities are crucially important in determining whether an insurrection will occur and what its likely outcome will be. However, the danger of psychological reductionism must be avoided.

There is only one correct way to utilize personality data in conjunction with social systems analysis, and that is through the macro/micro distinction. From the macroscopic perspective of the overall system, the analyst will consider the disequilibrium-induced variations in role performances and the policies of the various conflicting groups in relation to the functioning of the system, regardless of the *motivations* of the actors. In the case of the Taiping Rebellion in nineteenth-century China, for example, the analyst will consider how the ideology of the Taiping leader, Hung Hsiu-ch'üan, came to be accepted by millions of peasants as offering a way to resynchronize the system; he will ignore the fact that Hung was an epileptic and that this condition undoubtedly contributed in a major way to his behavior.[33] He will be interested to know what psychological needs may be met by subversive political activities for outcasts, déclassés, undesirables, and the "maladjusted," but his analytical focus directs him to how their social movements influence the system rather than to their psychological health. The analyst of a social system never decides a priori who is insane, a criminal, or a revolutionary in a system; he discovers that from his study of the social system.

The micro-analyst, conversely, is concerned with the distinction between behavior which is motivated by individual, childhood-derived personality needs and behavior which is motivated by disequilibrium-induced, personal tension among previously non-deviant actors. In a revolutionary situation, he will need to study both the personalities of revolutionary leaders and the tensions of their followers, and he must explain how the two complement each other. He must distinguish, as Wallace has done, between the "mazeway resynthesis" of the innovator (a stable reconstitution of the mazeway of an individual, often occurring under hallucinatory conditions and often reducible to personality factors) and the "hysterical conversion" of his followers (a reversible change in personality characteristics, e.g., the conversions of rank-and-file Nazis or Black Muslims).[34]

Although it is generally true that personality analysis must be oriented to the biography of a single individual, all generalizations about clusters of personalities are not ruled out. One of the main conceptual tools of the micro-analyst is that of "modal personality" or "national character," a statistical construct referring to "relatively enduring personality characteristics and patterns that are modal among the adult members of the society."[35] Unfortunately, older theories of modal personality were based almost exclusively on the replication-of-uniformity image of society, and they tended to view personality wholly as a function of a social system's culture. Today it is widely acknowledged that concepts of modal personality cannot offer a guide to the behavior of any particular person; they can only be used as statistical indicators of the behavioral propensities of a specific group of people.

When modal personality is understood in a statistical sense, it allows one to conceptualize differences in attitudes toward authority, tolerance of ambiguity, acceptance of variations among people, and so forth. Such information is directly relevant to studies of the disequilibrated social system. For example, in systems where individualism is a pronounced modal personality trait, much of the tension induced by disequilibrium will be tolerated through "inner migration" and comparable personality defense mechanisms. Similarly, the discovery that "authoritarian personalities" are modal in all or part of a social system is of direct relevance to the rise of authoritarian revolutionary associations, of both the right and the left, under disequilibrated conditions. Disequilibrium in a society always produces personal tension, but the amount and the form of this tension varies from society to society, and modal personality offers a way to study these differences.

Social psychologists create a particular conception of modal personality by collecting and analyzing data in three main areas: direct psychological reports taken from a sample of the population; psychological interpretations of cultural traits, such as folklore, mass media, and so forth, which reflect adult personality characteristics; and psychological analyses of a society's child-rearing norms. It is absolutely essential that information collected in this way be used in conjunction with macro systems analysis and with individual-specific micro analyses of important personalities in the system. Particularly in the study of revolutions, attention must be paid to the congruence between modal personality and a functional social system, the type of modal personality, the type of social system (i.e., the specific form of a value-environmental symbiosis), and the impact of a social system's disequilibrated conditions on personalities within the system. Later on in this book, we shall utilize one theorist's attempt to create modal personality categories in analyzing the psychological dimensions of revolution, and still later, we shall raise the personality problem again in trying to isolate indicators of systemic disequilibrium.

Another characteristic of the disequilibrated social system is the tendency for the society to fracture into polarized manifest interest groups as some members of the system begin to accept ideological alternatives to the old value structure. As we have already seen, all functional societies generate a hierarchy of statuses as a concomitant of solving their problems of role allocation and assignment. This network of stratification is stabilized through the envalued explanation of each status's position and through such homeostatic processes as social mobility. Under disequilibrated conditions, with the stabilizing effects of the value structure impaired, status protests may develop throughout the system, even when most statuses were not affected directly by the initial source of change. That is to say, latent interests in altering the *status quo*, interests which inhere latently in all subordinate statuses, tend to become manifest as the value structure and the division of labor progressively dissynchronize.

This phenomenon does not take place at once. The chief systemic mechanism militating against it is multiple role playing. Normally, a single individual will play numerous roles — worker, father, citizen, member of a recreational association, religious communicant, labor union member, and so forth — and under conditions of equilibrium the interests of one role will counterbalance the interests of another, keeping the actor's total status interests ambiguous. As Coser has observed, "One of the traditional Protestant arguments against Catholicism in this country, as well as one of the traditional arguments against Communists, is precisely that these organizations attempt to capture the total allegiance of their members, thus insulating them against the customary cross-conflicts of American society."[36] When a system becomes disequilibrated, multiple role playing still continues to prevent an immediate revolution or disintegration of the system, but its operations become considerably more vulnerable to attack.

As the disequilibrium of a social system becomes more acute, personal tensions are generated in all statuses. These tensions may be controlled by some people through internal psychological defense mechanisms, and the alienative sentiments of others may be dissipated through deviant behavior (e.g., fantasies, crime, mental disease, and psychosomatic illnesses).[37] However, with the passage of time, these mechanisms tend to lose their efficacy, and persons subject to highly diverse status protests will begin to combine with each other and with deviants generally to form a deviant subcultural group or movement.

Examples of this grouping of protesters are common. The union of retired military officers, physicians (particularly surgeons), frustrated politicians, functionless women, religious fundamentalists, taxpayers' groups, racists, and some businessmen into the so-called "radical right" in America is one. Another includes the *ad hoc* gathering of student idealists, Negro intellectuals, self-proclaimed pacifists, and some labor union members to form the anarchic left in contemporary America. A theoretical formulation of this phenomenon is Kurt Riezler's "psychological class," made up of outcasts, fools, and experts.[38]

The dynamic element which overcomes the effects of multiple role playing and which leads to the development of lines of cleavage is ideology. Without ideology, deviant subcultural groups, such as delinquent gangs, religious sects, and deviant patriotic associations, will not form alliances; and the tensions of the system, which led particular groups to form these associations, will be dissipated without directly influencing the social structure. Once persons whose latent interests have become manifest have an ideology, however, the society will tend to polarize into two groups: one group with an interest in maintaining the *status quo* and another with an interest in and an ideology for altering the *status quo*.

Let us explore the nature and the effects of ideology in greater detail. There are several different usages of the term "ideology," and they must be carefully distinguished if the concept is to have any analytic value. One such usage equates ideology with what we have been calling the value structure. Although Erik Erikson's interest in ideological constructs is directed almost exclusively to innovative ideologies (such as those of the Lutheran, Gandhian, and civil rights protest movements), his *definition* of ideology conforms more closely to the sociological conception of value structure: ". . . ideology [is] an unconscious tendency underlying religious and scientific as well as political thought: the tendency at a given time to make facts amenable to ideas, and ideas to facts, in order to create a world image convincing enough to support the collective and individual sense of identity. Far from being arbitrary or consciously manageable (although it is as exploitable as all of man's unconscious strivings), the total perspective created by ideological simplification reveals its strength by the dominance it exerts on the seeming logic of historical events, and by its influence on the identity formation of individuals."[39] Another theorist who uses ideology to refer to established values is Mannheim; he contrasts "ideology" — a stable structure of values — with "Utopia," which to him means an innovative belief system.

In contradistinction to the usage of either Erikson or Mannheim, we reserve the word ideology to refer to an *alternative* value structure, which becomes salient only under disequilibrated conditions and which is addressed to these disequilibrated conditions. An ideology, in this sense, may evolve into a value structure if it is instrumental in resynchronizing the system; but as an "ideology," it is always a challenger, an alternative paradigm of values. An ideology has inherent in its role of challenger certain special characteristics, some of which have been described by Parsons: "Ideologies combine an evaluative and an empirical element in the diagnosis of social situations. Because of evaluative pressures, they tend toward selectivity and sometimes outright distortion, both in stating the case of the proponents and attacking that of the opponents. It is typical that the former are pictured as actuated by the highest of idealistic motives, while the latter are guided by the grossest forms of self interest."[40]

As Parsons's definition suggests, ideologies perform various psychological functions for the management of personal tensions created by disequilibrated conditions. Seen from a micro perspective, ideologies attempt to relieve the tensions generated by disequilibrium, just as seen from a macro perspective, they attempt to show the way toward value-environmental resynchronization. Ideologies arise in disequilibrated systems as the competitors to an old value structure, and they define and explain the disequilibrated system in a way comparable to the value structure's definition and explanation of a functional system. As Geertz has argued on this point: "It is when neither a society's most general cultural orientations nor its most down-to-earth, 'pragmatic' ones suffice any longer to provide an adequate image of political process that ideologies begin to become crucial as sources of sociopolitical meanings and attitudes. In one sense, this statement is but another way of saying that ideology is a response to strain. . . . It is a loss of orientation that most directly gives rise to ideological activity, an inability, for lack of usable models, to comprehend the universe of civic rights and responsibilities in which one finds oneself located." [41]

Ideologies are incipient value structures, but they are not usually (and may never become) as developed and as inclusive as synchronized structures of values. Some ideologies will be very simple intellectual constructs which serve as psychological scapegoats, such as anti-Semitism, "Goldwaterism," Black Muslimism, or many "pacifist" doctrines (e.g., those which hold "warmongers," militarists, and munitions-makers responsible for most social ills).* These simple, tension-managing ideologies will rarely become sufficiently generalized to absorb more than a few groups of status protesters, but their more numerous appearance in society is a sound indicator of systemic disequilibrium. Ideologies are most typically crude rationalizations of a partially understood social situation, but it is possible that over time they may be

---

* Coser directly relates ideology, in this sense, to the strain resulting from instability in the stratification network. "Some types of anti-Semitism, as do other forms of prejudice, have important functions for those who suffer from 'degrouping,' that is, from a loss of cohesion in the society of which they are a part. Anti-Semitism provides a means for pseudo-orientation in an estranged world." *The Functions of Social Conflict* (Glencoe, Ill.: Free Press, 1956), p. 108.

perfected and revised to the point where they constitute both a program of action and an almost operable alternative paradigm of values (e.g., Marxism-Leninism).*

When an ideology is developed enough to be a full-blown revolutionary ideology, it will combine the ideas of "goal," "instrument," and "value." Such ideologies are what Wallace has called "goal cultures," or what we would call images of a new value-environmental symbiosis. They also define the means for reaching the goal — that is to say, they contain a "transfer culture," or "a system of operations which, if fully carried out, will transform the existing culture into the goal culture" (e.g., the seizure of power by a Leninist-type of communist party and the establishment of the "dictatorship of the proletariat").[42] Revolutionary ideologies are thus composed of a transfer culture and a goal culture, and several alternative ideologies are usually developed in a period of disequilibrium in an effort to overcome the deficiencies of the existing culture.

Ideologies are not policies. The latter are programs of action intended to achieve resynchronization, but they are informed and inspired by the desire to conserve parts of the old value structure and to avoid violence in the process of resynchronization. Ideologies are always replacements for the old value structure, even though they may derive from idealized versions of even earlier value structures, as in anarchistic revolutions or counter-revolutions. Since ideologies are anticipatory values, they are exclusivist in their orientation toward both the old value structure and competing ideologies. The advocates of an ideology will not enter into negotiations over the contents of their ideology since they regard themselves as representatives of superindividual claims, and for this reason it is normally difficult to routinize ideological competition within a system.

A special characteristic of that part of a revolutionary ideology outlining the transfer culture — i.e., the ideologically-defined methods for achieving the goal culture — is its imminentism. An

---

* In becoming a value structure, Marxism-Leninism adds a third hyphen-ated component, e.g., Marxism-Leninism-Stalinism, Marxism-Leninism-Titoism, Marxism-Leninism-Maoism, Marxism-Leninism-Castroism, and so forth.

ideology does not envisage postponing its realization to a later time or a superterrestrial existence; it is a program for immediate renovation in the here-and-now. This is not to say that a revolutionary ideology may not be built around a set of religious or metaphysical beliefs; all revolutionary "millenarian" ideologies, for example, are religious. But even they stress that the intervention of divine providence on the side of the revolutionaries is imminent and will produce a drastic, sweeping transformation of life as it is presently known in society.[43] Most revolutionary ideologies are frankly secular.

Because imminentism is only appropriate so long as the old value structure remains in being, a revolutionary ideology must rapidly divest itself of many of its imminentistic features if it successfully guides a revolution and then becomes the new value structure of the post-revolutionary society. As Parsons has written on this subject, "[There are] tensions involved in maintaining the ideology intact, including its utopian elements, and yet making the indispensable concessions to the exigencies of operating as a society. . . . A transcendental system of religious beliefs has an advantage over a secular ideology [as a stable value structure] in that it can project the *Ausgleich* of discrepancies into the transcendental sphere while for the secular ideology the future is the only recourse. Without this resource the really radical utopian ideology may well have to give way to pressure after a struggle." [44] In the process of transforming itself into a value structure, a post-revolutionary ideology will also greatly expand its range of definitions and explanations in accordance with its basic principles. It will also establish definitions of crime and sickness, and thereby divest the new system's authority statuses of the personal deviants who joined the movement under the guise of, or in the belief that they were, status protesters (e.g., Hitler's purge of Ernst Röhm and the SA in June 1934).[45]

Where do ideologies come from? They are created by individuals who may be motivated by personal psychological needs, life experiences, disequilibrium-induced tensions, or a combination of all these forces. Obviously, such ideologists may appear in periods in which the society is not disequilibrated, and in that case, the ideological constructs they create will circulate only among occupants of marginal statuses or will remain unknown to any group within the system. A social system becomes receptive to ideological attacks on its values only because it is laboring under disequilibrium. As Tocqueville has said, "In all periods, even in the Middle Ages, there had been leaders of revolt who, with a view to effecting certain changes in the established order, appealed to the universal laws governing all communities, and championed the natural rights of man against the State. But none of these ventures was successful; the firebrand which set all Europe ablaze in the eighteenth century had been easily extinguished in the fifteenth. For doctrines of this kind to lead to revolutions, certain changes must already have taken place in the living conditions, customs, and mores of a nation and prepared men's minds for the reception of new ideas."[46]

As we have repeatedly observed, it is the disequilibrated conditions produced by value and/or environmental change that make men receptive to ideologies. For ideologies to gain currency, regardless of the motives of the ideologist, the time must be, in Carlyle's phrase, "an era of prophets." "Here enters the fatal circumstance of Idolatry," he writes, "that, in the era of the Prophets, no man's mind *is* any longer honestly filled with his Idol or Symbol. Before the Prophet can arise who, seeing through it, knows it to be mere wood, many men must have begun dimly to doubt that it was little more. Condemnable Idolatry is *insincere* Idolatry. Doubt has eaten-out the heart of it: a human soul is seen clinging spasmodically to an Ark of the Covenant, which it half-feels now to have become a Phantasm. This is one of the balefulest sights. Souls are no longer *filled* with their Fetish; but only pretend to be filled, and would fain make themselves feel that they are filled. 'You do not believe,' said Coleridge; 'you only believe that you believe.' It is the final scene in all kinds of Worship and Symbolism; the sure symptom that death is now nigh. It is an equivalent to what we call Formulism, and Worship of Formulas, in these days of ours."[47]

Seen from the vantage point of social science, Carlyle's description accurately portrays the crisis of an incoherent value structure. However, we should remember that the ideologist or prophet only provides a more effective fetish. It would be unfounded to suggest that the resynchronization of a system in accordance with an ideology constitutes progress or movement toward a truer form of social organization. Resynchronization does reduce personal tension and lays down a foundation of trust which produces greater efficiency in the division of labor; from the point of view of systems theory, men in disequilibrated societies listen to prophets only in order to achieve these ends.

Given a high degree of generality and insight on the part of an ideology, it will spread beyond the single deviant group around its creator and attract many other persons trying to cope with disequilibrium-induced tensions. Such followers will not be equally motivated or have precisely the same interests, and the group attracted by an ideology may or may not be able to organize an effective revolutionary party. Given sufficient time, however, an ideology will cause the disequilibrated society to divide into one group of allies seeking to change the structure of the system and another seeking to maintain it. It is in this environment of change, tension, and power deflation that a system's leaders must act to bring about conservative change and to forestall revolution. It is to their actions and their potential contribution to the outbreak of revolution that we shall now turn.

5

Revolution

KARL POPPER once said, "Institutions are like fortresses. They must be well designed and properly manned."[1] This is certainly a sound observation, but it raises endless complications for the analyst of change and revolution. In practice, a well designed set of institutions can go a long way toward compensating for poor elite role performances, and conversely, a high order of political leadership will occasionally make the most rickety of institutions function extraordinarily well. On the other hand, perversely bad leadership often undermines an otherwise well-organized division of labor, and some social structures are so inappropriate under changing conditions that even the best leadership in the world cannot compensate for their deficiencies. Considerations of this sort demand that the analyst of revolution adopt a multi-disciplinary approach to the problems of political violence. Any attempt to reduce the phenomenon of revolution solely to social structure, or to political behavior, or to historical accident, is foredoomed to failure because it is superficial.

Machiavelli was one of the first modern political theorists to

point this out. In *The Prince*, he used three basic concepts to discuss the various problems of political leadership: *virtù, fortuna,*
and *necessita.* By *virtù,* he meant the mastery, i.e., the "virtu-
osity," that some men acquire over forces operative in political
situations; by *fortuna,* those events over which no human being
has any control; and by *necessita,* the limitations placed upon
human choice by the society in which political decisions must be
made. As he then went on to demonstrate, there can be nothing
but error in the practice of a Prince — or, by extension, in the
analysis of a social scientist — that relies exclusively upon either
virtue, or fortune, or necessity. All three must be combined.

Dorothy Emmet perpetuates Machiavelli's methodological insight when she argues that "no society [can] survive without
elements both of the conscious teleology of purpose and of the
unconscious teleology of function." According to her, as to
Machiavelli, the social analyst must "ask not only 'what are the
observable social results of this activity?' but [also] 'what are
these people trying to do?' "[2] A third element, which she omits
and which we must reintroduce from Machiavelli, is the effects of
capricious events — of *fortuna* — on a particular social situation
in which the political actors are behaving intentionally to achieve
certain definable goals.

The complicating element in all this is that, as Machiavelli also
knew, virtue, fortune, and necessity cannot be fully isolated —
that is to say, they are interdependent and mutually influencing
variables. For example, the likelihood that political leaders will
display high ability at any one time is directly affected by the
history of the social system's functioning during the preceding
years. Conversely, how the system functioned itself will have
depended to some extent upon the insight and acumen of political
leaders during non-crisis periods. Similarly, while fortune is
beyond the control of men, it may be influenced, or its influence
mitigated, by the actions of men. Mastery in politics is often accompanied by good fortune in the political sphere, whereas a
disequilibrated social system and narrow-minded, or weak, leadership seem to invite misfortune. Foreign wars coming on top of
domestic conditions of social change have often led to revolutions, but the occurrence of foreign wars at such times is not

wholly unforeseeable. As Machiavelli noted about that particular piece of *fortuna:* "When once the people have taken arms against you, there will never be lacking foreigners to assist them."[3]

Virtue, fortune, and necessity are thus interrelated, but they require separate analyses using different conceptual tools. The study of virtue requires that we identify the choices open to political actors and analyze both the self-conscious purposes and the underlying needs of these individuals. Machiavelli addressed himself to this problem by cataloguing what ought to be the purposes and the actions of a Prince who wishes to prosper; today social scientists do the same thing, although without prescriptive intent, using a form of decision-making analysis. In studying fortune, or unpredictability, social scientists analyze historical cases in a clinical search for patterns of the way in which fortune has intervened in various situations in the past. Necessity, or the limitations on choice established by the social system, requires still a third form of analysis. As we have already seen, here the problem is not so much the purposes or choices that men select — that is, man's own understanding of his social life — but the unintended consequences of the particular understandings and arrangements that men have chosen, or inherited, in organizing their interdependence. Here, in short, the method of analysis must be sociological.

Again, it must be stressed that these inquiries are not mutually exclusive. Political actors occasionally adopt policies which run counter to sociological realities (conceived as the social requisites for the continuation of a particular system with a particular social structure), and occasionally these policies succeed in changing the structure without destroying the system's equilibrium. Hence the study of the social setting of political action is not deterministic in the philosophical sense. On the other hand, politics as a homeostatic process is "the art of the possible," and the sociological study of politics aims at determining the limits of the possible in any given social system.

These observations on the methods of social science directly inform the present analysis of revolution. We are seeking, first, a theoretical formulation of the necessary and sufficient causes of a revolution and, second, to know why revolutions, when they do occur, sometimes succeed and sometimes fail. We believe that there are two clusters of mutually-influencing necessary, or remote, causes of any revolution. First, there are the pressures created by a disequilibrated social system — a society which is changing and which is in need of further change if it is to continue to exist. Of all the characteristics of the disequilibrated system, the one that contributes most directly to a revolution is *power deflation* — the fact that during a period of change the integration of a system depends increasingly upon the maintenance and deployment of force by the occupants of the formal authority statuses.*

The second cluster of necessary causes revolves around the quality of the purposeful change being undertaken while a system is disequilibrated. This quality depends upon the abilities of the legitimate leaders. If they are unable to develop policies which will maintain the confidence of non-deviant actors in the system and its capacity to move toward resynchronization, a *loss of authority* will ensue. Such a loss means that the use of force by the elite is no longer considered legitimate, although it does not necessarily mean that a revolution will occur at once. So long as the leaders can still use the army successfully to coerce social interaction, the system will continue to persist. However, the power deflation will approach maximum proportions, producing a "police state" (e.g., South Africa today).

The final, or sufficient, cause of a revolution is some ingredient, usually contributed by fortune, which deprives the elite of its chief weapon for enforcing social behavior (e.g., an army mutiny), or which leads a group of revolutionaries to *believe* that they have the means to deprive the elite of its weapons of coercion. In this study, such final, or immediate, causes of revolution are referred to as "accelerators." They are the pressures, often easily sustained in functional societies, which when they impinge on a society experiencing power deflation and a loss of authority immediately catalyze it into insurrection. They are also the factors which determine, when an insurrection does occur, whether or

* For an analysis of the concept of power deflation, see Chapter Two, pp. 27–33.

not the revolutionaries will succeed in establishing and occupying new statuses of authority.

The conditions generated by a disequilibrated social system — what in popular parlance are called "social problems" — can never in themselves be the sufficient causes of a revolution. What they do is to create demands that the system be adjusted, through political action, to the changed circumstances. While policies for adjusting the system are being created and implemented, phenomena such as rising rates of deviancy, increased status protests, the circulation of ideologies, and so forth, will appear. In order to control these and maintain some systemic integration under stress, the elite must use its legitimate means of force more frequently. But so long as confidence in future improvement is maintained among non-deviant actors, this increased use of force will be regarded as legitimate and tolerated as a necessary concomitant of social change. The authorities may even suppress an armed insurrection undertaken by an isolated group without bringing their authority into doubt (e.g., the suppression of an urban insurrection caused by temporary food shortages, extreme heat, and the like).

As Lucian Pye has commented on this point, "We [Americans] tend to suspect that any government confronted with a violent challenge to its authority is probably basically at fault and that significant numbers of rebels can only be mobilized if a people has been grossly mistreated. Often we are inclined to see insurgency and juvenile delinquency in the same light, and we suspect that, as 'there is no such thing as bad boys, only bad parents' so there are no bad peoples, only evil and corrupt governments. . . . Instead of the analogy of bad parents producing delinquent children, the classic British view has paralleled the belief that schoolboys will always misbehave if not controlled by the school master."[4] Whether or not Pye has accurately portrayed the British and American attitudes toward the authoritative use of force, he is correct in suggesting that the use of force in a power deflation, so long as it remains legitimate, can be rationalized. Well-socialized actors will continue to expect authorities to control deviancy during times of change.

The crucial question is whether or not non-deviant actors —

persons managing their disequilibrium-induced tensions in some private manner — continue to believe in the willingness and competence of the elite to resynchronize the system.* In order to maintain confidence in itself an elite must do two things: it must perceive that the system is disequilibrated, and it must take appropriate steps to restore equilibrium. *"Gouverner, c'est choisir,"* said former French Premier Pierre Mendès-France; and the choices that an elite makes in trying to govern during times of change directly affect whether or not that elite will become the target of revolution.

The revolution of 1848 offers us an example. According to historian Lewis Namier, "Count Galen, the Prussian Minister, wrote from Kassel on 20 January 1847: 'The old year ended in scarcity, the new one opens with starvation. Misery, spiritual and physical, traverses Europe in ghastly shapes — the one without God, the other without bread. Woe if they join hands!' "[5] What happened, however, was that the elites of continental Europe prevented urban demands for republican government and rural demands for altered rules of land tenure from joining hands. Namier writes: "The proletariat was defeated in Paris, [and] the peasants were bought off in the Habsburg Monarchy [through concessions]. The social forces behind the revolution of 1848, disjointed and insufficient from the very outset, were thus practically eliminated. What remained was the middle classes led by intellectuals, and their modern ideology with which they con-

---

* By "elite" we mean the group of actors who occupy the statuses of authority in a social system. The size of this group will, of course, vary from one social system to another. Karl Deutsch's definitions in this sphere provide a rough abstract picture of the size of an elite. He makes a ". . . three level distinction between a relatively small 'elite,' usually of less than 5 percent of the population; a broader set of 'politically relevant strata' or 'mobilized population' that, in addition to the elite, may often include anywhere between 10 and 90 percent of the population, depending on the political conditions, the currently salient issues, and the general level of social and economic development of a country; and a 'passive' or 'underlying' population that takes little or no part in politics, nor perhaps in any extended form of impersonal social communication." *The Nerves of Government, Models of Political Communication and Control* (New York: The Free Press of Glencoe, 1963), p. 40. Deviancy and overt status protests occur most frequently among the poorly socialized, underlying strata.

fronted the old established powers and interests. Foremost in that
ideology was their demand for a share in the government of States
to be remodelled in accordance with the national principle."[6]
Having perceived the situation, bought off the peasantry, and
neutralized the proletariat, the elites of Germany, Poland, Italy,
and parts of the Austrian Empire easily defeated the nationalist
insurrections. Had they taken no steps at all, they might have
succumbed to a general revolution; had they adopted more appropriate reforms, they might have avoided even the middle-
class revolts.

The courses of action open to a system's leaders during a power
deflation range from "conservative change" to its polar opposite,
"elite intransigence." The successful implementation of conservative change depends primarily upon two factors: the elite's
familiarity with social conditions, and its ability to determine
which elements of the value structure are indispensable to the
continuity of the culture. On the latter point, Pettee has written:
"Every myth [value structure] is embodied in a formal expression [institutionalized norms], and however much of eternal
truth may be in it, the expression itself is a temporal thing, related to time and circumstance. That expression may have been
nearly perfect, a quite unbetraying symbolic presentation of truth
for its age. But another age may find it ambiguous, erroneous,
frustrating [because values and the environment are no longer in
synchronization]. The task of the elite is then to revise the applied
code of good behavior of the myth, to deduce from the central
truth new rules of practical conduct."[7] If it can do this, the system will move toward resynchronization, the power deflation will
disappear, and no revolution will take place. Instead, we will
have an example of intentional, "conservative" change, such as
the New Deal in the United States, or the passage of the Reform
Bill of 1832 in England.

Elite intransigence, by contrast, always serves as a remote cause
of revolution. In its grossest form, elite intransigence is the frank,
willful pursuit of reactionary policies by an elite — that is, policies
which exacerbate rather than rectify a dissynchronized social
structure, or policies that violate the formal, envalued norms of the
system which the elite is charged with preserving. A recent ex-

ample of this latter kind of elite intransigence was the trial, on May 6 and 7, 1965, in Haynesville, Alabama, of the alleged murderer of Mrs. Viola Gregg Liuzzo, a white woman who was helping Negroes obtain their civil rights. According to criteria laid down by the values and norms of the system itself, the evidence against the accused, Collie LeRoy Wilkins, Jr., was conclusive (he was identified as the murderer by an accomplice, who was at the same time an informer for the Federal Bureau of Investigation). Nevertheless, the local jury deadlocked 10–2 and was dismissed. In this case, Wilkins was being judged only on a charge of first-degree manslaughter, the jury having already voted unanimously against a finding of first- or second-degree murder.

The Liuzzo trial was not an isolated case in which the elite betrayed the norms of the system. In 1964, two successive juries deadlocked in Mississippi in the murder trials of Byron de la Beckwith for the slaying of Medgar W. Evers. In 1959, after a masked mob of white men lynched a 23-year-old Negro, Charles Parker, in Poplarville, Mississippi, both federal and state grand juries refused to return indictments despite the collection of a great deal of evidence against the men. In 1955, a Mississippi grand jury did indict two men for the murder of a 14-year-old Negro boy, Emmett Till; but a jury acquitted them. In 1964, eighteen men, including Sheriff Lawrence A. Rainey, were indicted under a federal civil rights law for killing three civil rights workers in Philadelphia, Mississippi, but state authorities failed to return murder indictments against them. Also in 1964, a Georgia jury freed two Ku Klux Klan members accused of killing a U.S. Army reserve officer, Lemuel Penn, a Negro, while he was driving through the state.[8]

These cases illustrate a situation in which the social system has become disequilibrated but the elite, rather than attempting to preserve the main ingredients of the value structure, adopts policies which have the effect of discrediting the values themselves. Such actions disorient the behavior of *all* actors. The subordinate Negro population loses confidence in any solution to the disequilibrium short of violence, but the white beneficiaries of these policies also lose faith in the efficacy of the old values to provide the basis for an effective resynchronization. They too come to believe that violence is preferable to a restoration of the old order. So far, revolution in certain parts of the United States has been avoided only because many actors trust wider systemic authorities to mount legitimate actions against intransigent local elites, and because these local elites still possess overwhelming, although illegitimate, means of force. At the time of this writing, however, general policies of change in the direction of resynchronization are not so advanced that an accelerator would fail to elicit violent attempts to alter the social structure. The fact that a revolution has not yet occurred illustrates the principle that socialized actors will resort to violence only when all other means have been blocked.

Between the two poles of conservative change and elite intransigence, the policies of an elite in a disequilibrated system may vary from the barely adequate to the demonstrably incompetent. One of the most common "barely adequate" policies is the loosening of norms of social mobility in order to co-opt into the elite the actual or potential leadership of a group of organized status protesters. This often has the effect of resynchronizing the system under the old values, but it also constitutes an instance of social change because, in order to be effective, the criteria of the elite must be redefined to include the upwardly mobile leaders (e.g., the Lords' Reform, or the rise of *la noblesse de la robe*). As Pettee has observed, "The greater the degree of identity between the intrinsic and the socially recognized extrinsic elite, the less tension in society, all other things being equal."[9] The co-option of persons specially gifted with intellect has long been recognized as a sound anti-revolutionary measure since it neutralizes one obvious group of people who, if they are unreconciled to their status, are capable of creating a revolutionary ideology.

The incompetent policies of an elite are more often the result of its isolation than of its antisocial intentions. Nepotism, caste, dynastic decay, blocked channels of social mobility, and evolutionary changes in the norms governing authority may isolate an elite and prevent it from becoming fully aware of conditions in the society (e.g., the family government of the late President of South Vietnam, Ngo Dinh Diem). In these cases, the elite will be intransigent in effect — that is to say, it will adopt policies which are incommensurate with the problems it faces. If an accelerator intervenes, such an elite's efforts at reform will instantaneously be rendered irrelevant. An example was the government of China between the Boxer Rebellion of 1900 and the republican revolution of 1911–12. Led by the uneducated and, even according to the system's values, incompetent Empress Dowager, it promised reforms which it had no intention of realizing, created a revolutionary group by sending thousands of students abroad, and otherwise pursued policies of business as usual.

In some cases an elite will recognize and acknowledge its own incompetence in the face of disequilibrated conditions. One way for it then to avoid revolution is by formal, or virtual, abdication, which of course constitutes a kind of nonviolent social change (e.g., the termination of the Tokugawa government in Japan, or the Weimar authorities' virtual acquiescence in Hitler's radical program of change in 1933). Abdication by an elite may usher in changes of revolutionary magnitude, but it is not an instance of revolution if all actors, including the abdicating elite, agree to the change.

When a society is beset by a power deflation and a loss of authority, the sole basis of interaction becomes the primitive logic of deterrence, maintained by the elite's monopoly of armed force. Under these conditions, the threat of revolution is at its maximum. As Andrzejewski has concluded, "The incidence of rebellions largely depends on biataxy," a condition which he defines as: "A society in which the distribution of power and, consequently, of wealth, prestige and other desirable things . . . is settled by naked force, that is to say, by the use or threat of violence."[10] Such a society still may not experience a revolution. If the elite maintains intact its monopoly of force, the society may persist until values can be created and inculcated that will legitimatize the elite's status within it (many post-revolutionary societies, such as the Soviet Union prior to 1953, reveal this configuration). Of course, when a system's integration rests on armed force alone, the armed forces themselves must be greatly expanded, including secret police, which are used to terrorize — that is, to atomize — the population.

Even in cases where new values are never developed, the society may persist without revolution. In this case, it undergoes a long-term, secular decline brought on by its inability to generate even a modest level of systematic social interaction or to control the disequilibrium-induced personal tensions of its members. Slowly, but inexorably, such a social "system" will convert itself into a huge concentration camp, and this form of organization is unlikely to persist beyond the lifetime of the individual. As Tocqueville observed, "Even if [the French Revolution] had not taken place, the old social structure would nonetheless have been shattered everywhere sooner or later. The only difference would have been that instead of collapsing with such brutal suddenness it would have crumbled bit by bit. At one fell swoop, without warning, without transition, and without compunction, the Revolution effected what in any case was bound to happen, if by slow degrees."[11]

Given disequilibrated conditions and the elite's loss of authority, should some factor intervene to prevent the elite from maintaining its monopoly of force, a revolutionary insurrection will occur. There is surprising agreement among scholars on the final cause of a revolution — "It is that event," writes Gottschalk, "which demonstrates clearly that the conservative forces are no longer able to resist the revolutionary tide."[12] Peter Amann concurs: "Revolution prevails when the state's monopoly of power is effectively challenged and persists until a monopoly of power is reestablished."[13] Pettee also argues, "The human forces which create and maintain institutions have long been withdrawn. They have gone into new and attractive activities; for the most part they are in the new activities which contradict the old system, or into outright revolutionary activities, or into frivolity and dissipation. Under such conditions the mighty inertia of the existing institutions declines rapidly, though with almost no outward sign. The time comes when this inertia is no longer stronger in its control of behavior than the contradictory impulses of men. There the matter rests until some incident suddenly makes apparent the already real though latent situation."[14]

The event which triggers revolution in a society that is disequilibrated and that has a discredited base of authority is called an "accelerator" in this volume. Accelerators are occurrences that make revolution possible by exposing the inability of the elite to maintain its monopoly of force. They are not sets of conditions but single events — events that rupture a system's pseudo-integration based on deterrence. Accelerators always affect an elite's monopoly of armed force, and they lead either mobilized or potential revolutionaries to believe that they have a chance of success in resorting to violence against a hated system.

There are three different kinds of accelerators, each of them requiring separate analysis. The first kind includes factors that directly influence a system's armed forces — their discipline, organization, composition, or loyalty. When the necessary causes of revolution have been fulfilled — that is, when a society is biataxic due to a power deflation and a loss of authority — a break in the effectiveness of the armed forces will produce a revolution whether a revolutionary party exists or not. The second kind of accelerator is a component of the transfer culture of a revolutionary ideology; it is an ideological belief held by a protesting group that it can, for a variety of reasons, succeed in overcoming the elite's armed might. Examples include beliefs that God will intervene at a particular time on the side of the revolutionaries, that an attack on a barracks will cause the entire population to rally around the attackers (e.g., the Easter Rebellion, Dublin, 1916), that a general strike is an effective way to break the elite's coercive monopoly, that a secessionist movement will not be challenged by the elite, and so forth. The third kind of accelerator consists of special operations launched against an elite's armed forces by a group of conspirators who are pursuing a revolutionary strategy (e.g., guerrilla warfare). We shall postpone our discussion of such strategies until Chapter Eight.

An analysis of the political position of a system's armed forces always lies at the heart of any concrete study of a revolution. Since mounting a revolution involves the acceptance of violence in order to cause the system to change, revolutionaries must necessarily confront the actors who are entrusted, equipped, and trained to employ force within the system. "Armed insurrection in some form or other," writes Katharine Chorley, "is the classic method of making a revolution, and . . . it is bound to imply a clash with professionally trained troops equipped with all the gear of scientific warfare. History shows that, in the last resort, success or failure hinges on the attitude which those armed forces of the *status quo* government will take toward an insurrection. . . . Whatever government or party has the full allegiance of a country's armed forces is to all intents and purposes politically impregnable."[15]

In weighing the effects of an accelerator on a system's armed forces, the analyst must consider numerous factors. Is the army a caste-type of military elite or is it organized on the basis of some other exclusivist principle — i.e., a mercenary corps, a foreign army of occupation, or a domestic army recruited among an ethnic subgroup? Is it a mass army based on universal conscription? In what kinds of societies can a mass army be used to suppress a domestic revolt? What are the components of the armed forces available to the elite — e.g., external defense forces, militia, local police, and political police? Does the elite possess a separate armed unit that can be used against mutinous regular troops (e.g., the Nazi Party's SS, or the Red Army's cadets)? Does an accelerator impinge on all the armed forces or can the elite mobilize loyal troops to destroy the untrustworthy units? However, probably the single most important generalization to be made about the position of armies in revolutionary situations is that the officer corps and the rank and file have radically different attitudes toward the social system.

Because officers commanding armed forces are charged with enforcing a system's authority, in some systems the same people who occupy the statuses of authority also occupy the positions of military command (e.g., in feudal societies). In systems where military and authority statuses are separated, norms of role allocation and assignment must ensure that military officers do not suffer status insecurities that might cause them to exploit their status and violate the system's authority. If they do decide to exploit their status, officers can always impose their will on a system, so long as the army is united under them, because of the inability of any other group in the system to resist their armed might. One form of this usurpation of authority is an officers' revolution, but military intervention in politics is not always revolutionary. It may equally well take the form of an endogenous change in the division of labor, in which case it may create the disequilibrated conditions that will later contribute to a true revolution.

Military officers normally constitute at least a part of the *status quo* elite in a revolutionary situation. This is so because of the arrangements that are made in functional systems to avoid status protests among military officers. For example, until 1870 British military officers, particularly in the higher ranks, were recruited through the individual purchase of commissions. Despite the injustices whereby a rich man often bought command of a regiment over a more efficient but less affluent officer — and despite the fact that many British commanders were militarily incompetent as a result — the system was justified by political theorists (notably Burke) and by military leaders (notably the Duke of Wellington) as an effective measure against military insurrection. Parliament adopted the purchase system in 1683 after the Restoration, when a standing army was first formed and policy-makers were still troubled by the memory of Cromwell's major-generals. "Men were to become officers only if they could pay down a substantial sum for their commission; that is, if they were men of property with a stake in the country, not military adventurers."[16] British officers were "gentlemen," a characteristic that carried with it several disadvantages; however, Britain never suffered at the hands of a revolutionary army, and its army reliably put down any and all insurrections within the system.

Today most governments attempt to prevent military officers from exploiting their statuses through values and norms which stress service, separation from politics, and loyalty to the system as constituted. Great care is taken to socialize military officers in these special virtues, and most nations operate military academies for this purpose. However, since military loyalty under these circumstances rests primarily upon norms rather than interests, it is not surprising that during periods of change military officers often exhibit pronounced differences of opinion from the rest of a system's elite (e.g., Generals MacArthur and Edwin Walker in the United States). Military subordination to authority may be maintained homeostatically through norms whereby an officer must leave the armed forces and enter politics as a civilian if he wants to have a voice in public affairs (e.g., Generals Eisenhower and Maxwell Taylor).

In contrast to the officers' stratum, an army's rank and file is characterized by having an autonomous morale to the greatest extent possible in an integrated social system. Part of the logic of military efficiency (as well as contributing to the reliability of the statuses entrusted with the means of coercion) is to cut off troops from civilian interests so that they will accept their officers' orders unquestioningly. The effectiveness of a modern army — the use of both men and weapons as instruments — depends upon the creation of a least common denominator of ability in the men when they work together. All this is expressed in military science by the term "discipline." Disciplined, professional troops normally obey their officers, including the order to suppress armed insurrection.

In a situation of power deflation and loss of authority, a *status quo* elite can still maintain its position and the pseudo-integration of the system if it possesses a disciplined army commanded by officers who are themselves members of the elite. Insurrections that may occur in these situations will be put down by the army, and in so doing the army will exercise a deterring influence on all other potentially insurrectionary groups (e.g., the Sharpeville riot in South Africa in 1960). To the extent that the military-political elite makes its intention to use force truly credible, insurrections will not occur at all. However, armies are not always effective or loyal, and the analytical question therefore becomes what causes professionally-trained armed forces sometimes to lose their effectiveness?

Chorley lays down as a general rule that insurrections succeed "against the opposition of the regular armed forces [only] because these are for one reason or another prevented from making use of their full resources."[17] Fraternization with the populace is one factor that may weaken army unity and allow revolutionary sentiment to enter the ranks. Regardless of whether fraternizing troops actually join a revolution, the effects of fraternization may convince an elite that it cannot rely on the army to defend the *status quo*. Fraternization was a factor, for example, in the Hungarian Revolution of 1956; as the United Nations Special Committee on Hungary reported, "At times the Hungarians met with sympathy from Soviet troops. Soviet troops normally stationed in Hungary or in Romania had been affected by their surroundings. . . . Some Russian officers and soldiers appear to have fought and died on the Hungarian side." Significantly, the Committee also observed that "The forces used to repress the uprising in October were not exclusively forces which had been stationed in Hungary under the Warsaw Treaty."[18]

Another group of army-connected accelerators includes army mutinies wholly related to conditions of service and intra-military elite struggles due to factional differences. Such accelerators serve revolutionaries as windfalls. In 1929 and 1930 in China, for example, Mao Tse-tung took advantage of the revolts of generals within Chiang Kai-shek's government to launch his earliest guerrilla uprisings; and he later put part of the blame for the defeat of his early south China guerrilla bases on the communist failure to exploit the 1933 mutiny of Nationalist troops in Fukien province. Possibly the most famous example of this type of accelerator was the 1905 mutiny of the sailors on the battleship *Potemkin*, which converted the strikes of the Odessa workers into full-fledged revolt.

Accelerators affecting the army may consist of open mutinies or they may be disputes within the elite over the policies to be pursued in a disequilibrated situation. Indecisiveness on the part of the elite prevents it from giving coherent orders to the armed forces, including the order to suppress revolt, and this failure of command may be as valuable to revolutionaries as an internal mutiny. As Plato observed in the eighth book of the *Republic*, "Is it not a simple fact that in any form of government revolution always starts from the outbreak of internal dissension in the ruling class?"[19] The 1963 situation in South Vietnam provides a recent example of the effects of elite indecision. The United States and the government of Ngo Dinh Diem openly disagreed over whether to use force to suppress Buddhist protests against religious discrimination. The effect of the dispute was to make the armed forces unreliable, to stimulate the population of Saigon to insurrection, and eventually to lead the army to revolt against its government.

Of all the accelerators directly affecting the armed forces, by far the most important is defeat in war. This is the one occurrence that dissolves even well-trained military formations, and from a restricted perspective, revolution in modern times can almost be considered an invariable complication of international conflict. Chorley emphasizes the consequences of defeat above all others: "Experience proves that on the whole the rank and file will never disintegrate on their own initiative through the impact of direct political emotion. Some other and stronger solvent is required. The supreme solvent for the disintegration of the rank and file is an unsuccessful war. . . . There can be little doubt that under modern conditions the last stages of an unsuccessful war provide the surest combination of circumstances for a successful revolutionary outbreak."[20] Sometimes an elite has been able to mobilize enough loyal forces to put down a domestic insurrection even after a defeat in war, but the most important successful revolutions of the past century were all accelerated by the incapacitation of the armies of *status quo* elites in foreign wars. Examples include France, 1871; Russia, 1905 and 1917; Hungary, Germany, and Turkey, 1918; the overthrow of Mussolini, 1943; the anti-colonial revolts in French and Dutch colonies after World War II; and China and Yugoslavia during World War II.[21]

Whereas the first class of accelerators, such as defeat in war, directly affects the armed forces of an elite, the second class of accelerators consists of beliefs that the army *can be crippled* if a particular course of action is pursued. These beliefs or theories held by revolutionaries about their chances of success may or may not have any empirical validity. If they are not valid and an insurrection is attempted, *ceteris paribus*, it will be defeated (e.g., the Boxer Rebellion in China, where the rebels believed that they were immune from the effects of bullets). Even revolutionaries certain of their success may approach the actual staging of the revolution as a calculated risk and launch it under the guise of legal or semilegal activities in order to test the resolve of the elite and its armies (e.g., strikes, parades, mass meetings, and so forth). Similarly, revolutionaries will sometimes incite crowds to riot in order to test the structures of deterrence. Nevertheless, we have "no instance of a revolutionary strike which issues in armed insurrection succeeding in an overthrow of the existing system of government,"[22] and the more rational approach to toppling an elite defended by a reliable army is through a carefully planned coup d'état or through some *strategy* of revolution (see Chapter Eight).

Whatever the type of accelerator that impinges on a revolutionary situation, all accelerators have the same effect. They are events that functional societies can normally sustain without producing either a power deflation or a loss of authority, but which in disequilibrated societies lead men to believe that coercion can no longer be maintained over them. The classic example occurred in Petrograd in March 1917. Some 200,000 demonstrators, consisting of women and workers locked out of the Putilov Metal Factory, marched through the streets. Upon being given the order to fire into the crowd, the soldiers of the Volinsk Regiment fired into the air, thereby ending the monopoly of force of the Russian autocracy. Other units mutinied, the people sacked the headquarters of the Okhrana, and revolutionaries stormed into the prison fortress of St. Peter and St. Paul. Defeat in war was the accelerator that caused the soldiers to refuse their orders, and this refusal in turn produced the first successful Russian revolution of the modern age.

Up to this point, we have analyzed revolution from a macroscopic, or systemic, perspective — that is to say, we have avoided considering the motives and personality changes of the participants in a revolution. Our attention has been directed solely to various configurations of the system and to the malfunctioning of certain essential processes which, when they coincide, result in revolution. The principle which emerges from this analysis is that power deflation, plus loss of authority, plus an accelerator produces revolution (the chart on page 106 portrays graphically the relationship between these elements).

Now let us alter the perspective and explore one theorist's attempt to provide a microscopic model of the processes of revolution. Anthony Wallace does not use the term "revolution," but instead speaks of "revitalization" — a psychological equivalent of revolution, which he defines as a "deliberate, organized attempt by some members of a society to construct a more satisfying cul-

Figure 5-1   The Causes of Revolution

Sources of Change

Cause changes in structure of values, or pattern of the division of labor, or both

a) Exogenous value-changing, e.g., rise of external reference groups

b) Endogenous value-changing, e.g., religious innovation

c) Exogenous environment-changing, e.g., foreign conquest

d) Endogenous environment-changing, e.g., technological innovation

The Disequilibrated Social System

Structure of Values | Symbolic interpretations of Social Action

Dissynchronous

Failure to Fulfill Functional Requisites
1. Incoherent Socialization
2. Inappropriate ensemble of roles
3. Dissensus on goals
4. Failure to resolve conflicts peacefully

Relationship

Division of Labor | Pattern of Adaptation to the Environment

Routine homeostasis fails to create a new synchronization between value structure and pattern of environmental adaptation

Status Protesters — Interest in recasting the status hierarchy

The Decision-Making Arena in Power Deflation

Elite Courses of Action
1. Conservative change
2. Co-option of Status Protesters
3. Business as Usual
4. Intransigence

Status Protesters — Interest in restoration of old status hierarchy

Accelerator — Breaches logic of deterrence based on force

Loss of Authority (the result of the course of action chosen by the elite)

Integration of System Maintained by Use of Force

Revolutionary Insurrection — Its outcome depending on the attitudes of the armed forces and/or the validity of the transfer culture

TIME

ture by rapid acceptance of a pattern of multiple innovations."[23] In an earlier article on revitalization movements, he states that the term revitalization includes phenomena of change such as "revolutions," "mass movements," "nativistic movements," "charismatic movements," and so forth.[24]

The most significant characteristic of Wallace's idea of revitalization is that it is personality-oriented. "Under conditions of disorganization," he writes, "the system, *from the standpoint of at least some of its members,* is unable to make possible the reliable satisfaction of certain values which are held to be essential to continued well-being and self-respect. The mazeway of a culturally disillusioned person, accordingly, is an image of a world that is unpredictable, or barren in its simplicity, or both. His mood (depending on the precise nature of the disorganization) will be one of panic-stricken anxiety, shame, guilt, depression, or apathy."[25] The pressures which bring about these psychological states are, in Wallace's formulation, roughly equivalent to our sources of change — that is, they are endogenous or exogenous pressures on either values or the division of labor that disequilibrate a functionally integrated social system.

When people are suffering from panic-stricken anxiety, shame, guilt, depression, and so forth, as a result of systemic disequilibrium, they will carry out a revitalization movement or the whole society will slowly disintegrate. One of the problems of Wallace's conceptualization, however, is that he does not specify the sufficient, or final, causes of a revitalization movement. The particular psychological states which he describes are not in themselves sufficient to bring about a revitalization movement, since homeostatic or purposive processes of change might equally well relieve them. Since Wallace argues that revitalization is an extreme form of rapid change, we may infer that he assumes all other remedies for overcoming mazeway disorganization have been exhausted, thereby bringing the psychological needs of the actors to the threshold of revitalization. Without such a qualification, Wallace would be arguing that *all* social change occurs via revitalization, and he certainly does not believe that.

Given the condition of a disequilibrated social system, with its psychodynamic dimension of severely disorganized mazeways,

Wallace proceeds to conceptualize the stages through which actors pass in revitalizing their culture. He establishes various categories within which modal personality data can be fitted; and his formulation is probably the best abstract model in contemporary social science of the nature and cause of personality change during a revolutionary movement.

His formula consists of five stages. The first is a benchmark model of the integrated social system, which Wallace calls the "steady state" and which he defines as a social system in equilibrium. Change may occur while the system retains this configuration, but it is change of the evolutionary variety. The primary psychological characteristic of this period is that mazeway disorganization and the resulting internal tensions remain within tolerable limits for most individuals. Deviant behavior occurs among persons who are socially (i.e., through faulty socialization) or physically (i.e., through congenital malformation of the mazeway) incapable of managing the stress that exists routinely in their particular systems. "Occasional incidents of intolerable stress," says Wallace, "may stimulate a limited 'correction' of the system, but some incidence of individual ill-health and criminality are accepted as a price society must pay."[26]

When a source, or sources, of change disequilibrate this steady state, the system enters the second period, "increased individual stress." In this stage, "Anomie and disillusionment become widespread. . . . Crime and illness increase sharply in frequency as individualistic asocial responses."[27] Actually, Wallace may go too far toward suggesting that the social system and individual personalities change in a one-to-one ratio with each other. During this initial period of disequilibrium, many of the resulting psychological tensions will probably be managed through internal defense mechanisms and hence will be disguised. We should expect to see only slight rises in the rates of crime and mental illness, and even these changes may go unnoticed due to increasing dissensus over the precise definitions of crime and deviancy. A more likely indicator of stress during this period is the increased production and circulation of ideological constructs for rationalizing the new stresses.

So long as equilibrium is not restored, the system will proceed to the third stage, "cultural distortion." Here the tensions induced by disequilibrium become fully manifest, and the behavior resulting from them is measurable. "Some members of the society attempt, piecemeal and ineffectively, to restore personal equilibrium by adopting socially dysfunctional expedients."[28] These expedients may include alcoholism, attacking scapegoats, venality among public officials, breaches of sexual and kinship norms, hoarding, and so forth. Moreover, during this period the society will begin to divide into ideologically-oriented interest groups. Various groups will accept tension-managing constructs which may offer some sense of reorientation, but which, because of their crudity, cannot form the basis for reintegrating the whole system without extensive modification. Examples of the types of groups that appear during stage three are the Ku Klux Klan, the John Birch Society, the Minutemen, White Citizens' Councils, and the Black Muslims.

This stage finally gives way to "the period of revitalization" — what we would call the period of revolution. There is nothing inevitable about the occurrence of a revitalization movement. As Wallace acknowledges, "Once severe cultural distortion has occurred, the society can with difficulty return to a steady state without the institution of a revitalization process."[29] The possibility of conservative change thus remains open, although it obviously involves difficulties. If conservative change does not occur and no revitalization takes place either, "The society is apt to disintegrate as a system: the population will either die off, splinter into autonomous groups, or be absorbed into another, more stable, society" (e.g., several American Indian tribes, such as the ones described by Theodora Kroeber in her book *Ishi in Two Worlds*).[30]

Wallace breaks down the stage of revitalization into six requisite functions. First is the "formulation of a code," or what we have called the creation of a revolutionary ideology. The code is a prescription, meeting the psychological needs of the disoriented individuals, which tells them two things about the culturally distorted system: what to do to change it and what to replace it with in the future. These two functions are performed, respectively, by what Wallace calls the "transfer culture" and the "goal culture." Whether or not the goal culture can ever be achieved, its psychological importance is immense, for it opens up the possibility of liberation from the disturbing reality within which people have been trying to orient themselves.

The second requirement of a revitalization movement is communication, or the preaching of the code by its formulators with the aim of making converts. The formulators themselves will have experienced what Wallace calls "mazeway resynthesis" — a stable, irreversible conversion, characteristic of prophets. The converts, those who join the prophet's movement, will undergo "hysterical conversion," a form of personality change equivalent to that described by Eric Hoffer in *The True Believer*. Hysterical conversion may last for years, but it does require periodic reinforcement and is reversible.

Wallace's third and fourth requirements, organization and adaptation, refer to needs generated by small-group dynamics. "The tricornered relationship between the formulators, the disciples, and the mass followers is given an authoritarian structure . . . by the charismatic quality of the formulator's image." [31] This means simply that the people united by an ideology go on to organize themselves as a hierarchically-structured revolutionary association, regardless of the ultimate values to which they subscribe. "Adaptation" occurs as the transfer culture is hardened into a program of action. The revolutionary association now displays hostility not only toward its ideologically-defined enemy but also toward non-participating but ideologically-included members of the action party. Such persons will be branded as "traitors" (e.g., "Uncle Toms," "labor aristocrats," "social fascists," "running dogs," etc.).

These four requirements culminate in "cultural transformation" — the overt attempt to implement the transfer culture. Whatever form this may take — revolutionary war, coup d'état, general strike, or urban insurrection — if it is successful, it "will be attended by the drastic decline of the quasi-pathological individual symptoms of anomie and by the disappearance of the cultural distortion." [32] Assuming that the initial attempt at cultural transformation succeeds, the final task of a revitalization movement becomes "routinization." The focus of the movement shifts from innovation to maintenance, with the attendant development of norms to meet all the system's functional requisites. The surest sign that routinization is occurring is the elimination of those disciples and hysterical converts who are not able to reverse their revolutionary commitments. Hannah Arendt has pointed to the irony of this situation: "If foundation was the aim and end of revolution, then the revolutionary spirit was not merely the spirit of beginning something new but of starting something permanent and enduring: [however,] a lasting institution, embodying this spirit [i.e., the spirit of innovation and beginning] and encouraging it to new achievements, would be self-defeating. From which it unfortunately seems to follow that nothing threatens the very achievements of revolution more dangerously and more acutely than the spirit which has brought them about."[33] With routinization the system moves from the period of revitalization into Wallace's final conceptual stage, that of the new steady state.

There are several difficulties with Wallace's theory, but they are chiefly errors of omission rather than of commission (e.g., the failure to specify immediate causes), and they can be overcome by using the theory in conjunction with a macro-systemic conception of revolution. The great virtue of the theory is that it portrays what happens to individual thought and behavior as a social system becomes progressively disequilibrated, and it provides a tentative scheme for correlating stages of systemic change with stages of personality change. Such correlations are essential if we are ever to develop statistical measures of the degree to which a system is disequilibrated based on direct observation of human behavior.

Wallace summarizes his findings concerning personality stress during systemic disequilibrium in the form of a "principle of conservation of cognitive structure." This principle has three components, the first of which is that "The individual will not abandon *any* particular conception of reality (including, therefore, his culturally standard conceptions), even in the face of direct evidence of its current inutility, without having had an opportunity to construct a new mazeway."[34] This is a psychodynamic corollary of our fundamental premises that societies enjoying value-environmental synchronization are stable, that a disequilibrating source of change produces attempts to adapt prior to a resort to violence, and that revolution is purposeful, goal-oriented behavior, intended to overcome dissynchronization.

It is interesting to compare Wallace's formulation of this point with Kuhn's analysis of organized scientific research. Kuhn argues that a scientific "community" also depends upon the existence of a nature-defining paradigm, which scientists participating in a discipline jointly share (e.g., the Newtonian or Einsteinian paradigms). Given the existence of such an explanatory and definitive paradigm (in social systems, a value structure), "Novelty ordinarily emerges only for the man who, knowing *with precision* what he should expect, is able to recognize that something has gone wrong. Anomaly appears only against the background provided by the paradigm. . . . The decision to reject one paradigm is always simultaneously to accept another, and the judgment leading to that decision involves the comparison of both paradigms with nature *and* with each other. . . . Paradigm-testing occurs only after persistent failure to solve a noteworthy puzzle has given rise to a crisis. And even then it occurs only after the sense of crisis has evoked an alternative candidate for paradigm."[35] This alternative paradigm Wallace would call a goal culture and we would call a revolutionary ideology.

Wallace's second and third components of the principle of conservation of cognitive structure follow directly from his first: "(2) initial confrontation of the individual with evidence of inutility [anomaly, disequilibrium] will arouse an anxiety-denial syndrome, and this anxiety-denial response may continue for a considerable period of time; [and] (3) it is easier for the individual to abandon a conception if substitutes are offered and models of new mazeways are presented, than if the abandonment must be made 'blind.' "[36] We are inclined to state component three more positively: without an alternative value structure, the old system will simply destroy itself as the members futilely persist in their familiar but now inappropriate roles, norms, and statuses.

Having discussed revolution from two perspectives of contemporary social science — that of social systems theory and that of the psychology of culture change — let us now turn to a third and contrasting perspective on revolution, namely, the viewpoint of political philosophy. Our purpose in introducing this material is to point out some of the similarities that exist between our social science analyses and certain generalizations about revolution that have been preserved in the traditions of political philosophy. Since all three perspectives attempt to explain the same behavior, to the extent that the three resulting explanations tend to coincide we have a somewhat greater assurance that we have been conceptualizing revolutionary conditions accurately. The two political philosophers we shall consider are one from the tradition of Western philosophy, John Locke, and the other a contemporary theorist, Hannah Arendt.

Locke's theory of rebellion is similar to that of contemporary social systems analysis, except that he conceives of only one major source of revolutionary conditions: tyrannous behavior by a ruler or a legislature. Having thus narrowed his focus, he most often uses the term rebellion, rather than revolution, and he tends to think of the changes brought about by rebellion as restorative or preservative instead of innovative. Locke's theory of rebellion grows directly out of his theory of the "good" (we would say "functional") society. He understands the purpose of society to be the avoidance of a state of war, and he acknowledges that men must refrain from their pre-political right to employ force in their own interest while they are living within civil society. In *The Second Treatise of Civil Government* (1690), he wrote: "The reason why men enter into society is the preservation of their property; and the end why they choose and authorize a legislative is that there may be laws made and rules set as guards and fences to the properties of all the members of the society, to limit the powers and moderate the dominion of every part and member of the society; for since it can never be supposed to be the will of the society that the legislative should have a power to destroy that which every one designs to secure by entering into society, and for which the people submitted themselves to legislators of their own making. Whenever the legislators endeavour to take away and destroy the property of the people, or to reduce them to slavery under arbitrary power, they put themselves into a state of war with the people who are thereupon absolved from any further obedience, and are left to the common refuge which God hath provided for all men against force and violence." [37]

Some critics of Locke have supposed that his formulation allows for frequent and capricious resorts to rebellion, since he appears to have an extremely instrumentalist understanding of political organization — i.e., as a form of organization to which social actors give their support only so long as it protects their property. While under the regimen of political institutions, according to Locke, the people retain a separate, apolitical right — based on "a law antecedent and paramount to all laws of men"[38] — to judge the acts of their governors (the "legislative"). We must not suppose, however, that Locke believed people had a right to revolution. "This I am sure: whoever, either ruler or subject, by force goes about to invade the rights of either prince or people and lays the foundation for overturning the constitution and frame of any just government is highly guilty of the greatest crime I think a man is capable of."[39] Moreover, according to Locke people do not want to revolt against their government. "Such revolutions happen not upon every little mismanagement in public affairs. Great mistakes in the ruling part, many wrong and inconvenient laws, and all the slips of human frailty will be borne by the people without mutiny or murmur."[40] What, then, are the conditions under which rebellion is justified? Only, as Locke said, in the event of the return of war.

In order to make sense out of Locke's idea of the return of war, we must look in his work for concepts similar to our "power deflation" and "loss of authority." "Force," writes Locke, "is to be opposed to nothing but unjust and unlawful force."[41] Unlawful force is the opposite of the authoritative use of force, and Locke's understanding of the concept of authority leads to one of the more unusual aspects of his theory — namely, his notion that the original betrayer of authority, the tyrant, is the one who actually "rebels," and not the people who overthrow him by force following this betrayal. Authority is a complementary relationship, bestowing rights and obligations on those who obey and also on those who command. As Locke says, "Rebellion being an opposition, not to persons, but to authority which is founded only in the constitutions and laws of the government, those, whoever they be, who by force break through, and by force justify their violation of them, are truly and properly rebels; for when men, by entering into society and civil government, have excluded force and introduced laws for the preservation of property, peace, and unity amongst themselves, those who set up force again in opposition to

the laws do *rebellare* — that is, bring back again the state of war —
and are properly rebels."[42]

The occupant of a status of authority who exploits his authority
thereby loses his authority. His exercise of force becomes illegitimate. "When a king has dethroned himself," explains Locke, "and
put himself in a state of war with his people, what shall hinder
them from prosecuting him who is no king, as they would any
other man, who has put himself in a state of war with them?"[43]
Social interaction loses its social quality in the state of war, and
relations among men are once again settled solely through a calculus of force.

Given Locke's conception of the act of rebelling, we can see
how similar his theory is to the conclusions of social systems
analysis. Clearly, he conceives of society as a moral community,
and he regards the use of force within it as the last resort, as the
recourse of men whose reason is exasperated. The problem then
becomes what causes the occupants of the statuses of authority to
"rebel" in the first place. Locke is peculiarly silent on this subject.
He cites a series of conditions that typify the illegitimate exercise of
authority — breach of trust, misuse of funds, rigged elections —
but he identifies the causes of these conditions only as "ambition,
fear, folly, or corruption."[44] Locke thus imagines that the only
possible sources of change are endogenous mutations in the division of labor, and he has no theory at all to explain change toward
an unprecedented equilibrium. Rebellion for him stands at the extreme end of homeostatic processes and is undertaken only to control venality and to return the system to its original, envalued
configuration. Locke's theory of rebellion contributes to a general
understanding of political violence, but it is incapable of explaining all violent attacks by a people against their governors.

Hannah Arendt's language is similar to Locke's, but she differs
from him in being interested in *revolution* — the use of violence to
found new political communities. Her theory is a complement to
Locke's analysis of the rebellious, or restorative, form of political
violence. Arendt agrees with Locke that the most fundamental
cause of revolution is a loss of authority, but she means something
more general by authority than he did. Whereas Locke conceived
of authority chiefly as the contractual understandings achieved by

men in society for the purpose of avoiding the return of war and protecting their property, Arendt roots authority in a structure of values — in symbols which unite men by providing explanations of life for those who share them. Although her analysis is culture-bound, being wholly restricted to "Western" communities, her examples of the loss of authority all refer to losses of the power of value structures to unite people and to legitimatize authority among them.

"It may ultimately turn out," she writes, "that what we call revolution is precisely that transitory phase which brings about the birth of a new, secular realm. But if this is true, then it is secularization itself, and not the content of Christian teachings, which constitutes the origin of revolution."[45] Although Arendt does not go into the forces of change that led to secularization, she is acutely concerned with the consequences of the breaking up of the medieval symbiosis between universal Christian values and a division of labor based in part on them. This rupture destroyed the old bases of legitimate political authority and thereby generated a long series of changes and revolutions aimed at establishing some new basis of authority. The earliest, post-medieval attempts, she believes, failed in this respect: "European absolutism in theory and in practice, the existence of an absolute sovereign whose will is the source of both power and law, was a relatively new phenomenon; it had been the first and most conspicuous consequence of what we call secularization, namely, the emancipation of secular power from the authority of the church. . . . Absolutism . . . seemed to have found, within the political realm itself, a fully satisfactory substitute for the lost religious sanctions of secular authority in the person of the king or rather in the institution of kingship. But this solution, which the revolutions soon enough were to unmask as a pseudo-solution, served only to hide, for some centuries, the most elementary predicament of all modern political bodies, their profound instability, the result of some elementary lack of authority."[46]

Whether or not one agrees with Hannah Arendt that the absolutist regimes were inherently unstable, it is clear that by loss of authority ("the authority of the church") she is referring to a phenomenon closely comparable to our conception of a social system laboring under the effects of an incoherent value structure. She does not discuss in detail why the authority of the church once did provide a basis for a stable political community, but her understanding of the need for value sharing as the basis of community is identical to that discussed in this book in the language of the social system.

Turning to revolution itself — to the response generated by this "elementary lack of authority" — Arendt describes it as an act of "liberation," and she envisages a successful revolution in terms of the "foundation of freedom." "Violence," she writes, "is no more adequate to describe the phenomenon of revolution than change; only where change occurs in the sense of a new beginning, where violence is used to constitute an altogether different form of government, to bring about the formation of a new body politic, where the liberation from oppression aims at least at the constitution of freedom can we speak of revolution."[47] By liberation, she means the "passionate hatred of masters, the longing of the oppressed for liberation."[48] Although she says at one point that this longing is as old as human history, such a statement would appear to contradict her idea of authority. It is precisely because the religious bases of authority no longer explain and make tolerable the status hierarchy that the oppressed come to think of themselves as oppressed and to long for liberation. Thus, by the phrase "longing for liberation," she appears to mean something equivalent to the desire for a reduction in the tensions experienced by people living in a disequilibrated social system.

Arendt argues that a people longing for liberation may be provoked to "blind violence," or mere rebellion, and that this kind of behavior must be carefully distinguished from true revolution. While the longing for liberation may be a prerequisite for revolution, revolution also involves purpose. The revolutionaries must possess an ideology of the future, an alternative conception of the bases of authority. Hannah Arendt thinks that this ideology can take only one form; to her a popular desire for liberation is revolutionary only if it is informed by the "central idea of revolution, which is the foundation of freedom."[49] And, she adds, "Political freedom, generally speaking, means the right 'to be a participator in government,' or it means nothing."[50]

Although one may be willing to grant Arendt her definition of political freedom, there have been genuine revolutions that have had different goal cultures. Freedom, in her sense, was not the central idea of the Chinese Revolution of 1949, and it was certainly a true revolution according to all of her other criteria. Moreover, by freedom does Arendt mean only political participation, or does it also involve certain so-called checks and balances over the various occupants of the statuses of authority? If so, does the theory, held by some sociologists, that all government is oligarchic — the so-called "iron law of oligarchy" — make all revolutions in the name of freedom hopeless? We raise these questions not to answer them, but to indicate the extreme imprecision and narrowness of Arendt's idea of freedom used to *define* revolution.

From the perspective of a general theory of revolution, we must assume that Arendt is using the "foundation of freedom" as an elaborate example, or archetype, of what we have been calling "revolutionary ideology" or "goal culture." In order for the desire for liberation to take a genuine revolutionary form, she appears to be saying, the revolutionaries must have some intellectual construct, some vision, of how they want to recast society and install authority within it. Freedom, in this context, becomes the name of a particular pattern of relations of authority — one that Arendt believes the American revolutionaries successfully established and that the French Revolution failed to found.

Hannah Arendt's analysis, when it is read as a case study of an ideal type of revolution, coincides with the social science interpretations of revolution we have explored earlier. The Arendt perspective is too restricted, however, even when generalized in the present manner. She is correct in her belief that revolution is not mere change, but it is one form of change, and in order to understand revolution's occasional attractiveness as an alternative, it must be studied as part of the general phenomenon of social change.

6

Measuring disequilibrium

I T IS intrinsically impossible to construct a statistical measure that will predict the occurrence of a revolution. Because of revolution's multivariant causation — power deflation, plus loss of authority, plus an accelerator — we can only hope to discover measures of the disequilibrated social system, i.e., of the potentially revolutionary situation. As Arnold Feldman has observed, "Revolutions represent the extreme manifestation of social and political strains and tensions that are always present in some degree. Any attempt to measure the likelihood of revolution should therefore encompass the social sources of strains and tensions present in the several societies [subsystems] and the social conditions that either encourage or balance extreme acts among the contending forces. . . . The likelihood of revolutions is a function of both positive or conflict-generating factors and negative or conflict-controlling factors."[1] For reasons analyzed earlier, any attempt to measure revolutionary potential is simultaneously an attempt to measure the potential for other kinds of social change.

Nevertheless, efforts should be undertaken to construct an index of disequilibrium in a social system. Ideally, this index would portray the magnitude of dissynchronization between the structure of values and the social division of labor, thereby indicating the potentiality for termination of a system due to its failure to fulfill its functional prerequisites. Such a measure is needed on both theoretical and practical grounds. From the standpoint of theory, a statistical measure of disequilibrium would help to overcome the tendency toward tautology in practical applications of systems theory. Systems analysts of revolution are all too often guilty of arguing that disequilibrium is a prerequisite for revolution but that a system is known to be disequilibrated only because a revolution has occurred. If disequilibrated conditions do promote revolutions, they can and must be measured independently of the actual occurrence of revolutions. Practically speaking, an index of disequilibrium would provide a means of warning a legitimate elite of the possibility of revolution, thereby alerting it to the need for both policies of social change and military counter-insurgency preparations.

We do not yet have a single measure of disequilibrium, and I have neither the requisite statistical knowledge nor the data to construct such an index. In this chapter instead we shall discuss several indicators of disequilibrium that should be included in such an overall index and shall illustrate how they might have been used to predict historical, potentially-revolutionary conditions. Our purposes are both to clarify further the configuration of the disequilibrated system and to explore the adequacy of present statistics in offering meaningful guides to systemic disequilibrium. Some useful work has already been done along these lines — for example, W. W. Rostow's attempt to correlate economic fluctuations with political instability in nineteenth-century England, and Ronald Ridker's article, "Discontent and Economic Growth."[2] However, the usefulness of mere compilations of statistics concerning revolutions on a supra-systemic, comparative basis is questionable. Since revolution is a highly contingent phenomenon, analyses that divorce it from its contingent, causative circumstances within a particular disequilibrated social system can be of no theoretical interest.[3]

We have already discussed several indicators of disequilibrium.

Wallace suggested that increased rates of drunkenness, venality, breaches of sexual norms, and so forth, are marks of the early stages of cultural distortion; and clearly an attempt to define and count the appearance of tension-managing interest groups would be relevant to measuring disequilibrium. In this chapter we shall focus on the following potential symptoms of disequilibrium: suicide rates, heightened ideological activity, the military participation ratio, and the possible correlation between general and particular crime rates and disequilibrium.

Suicide is the most intriguing and complex single indicator with which social scientists have attempted to measure a social system's integration. Durkheim gave classical formulation to its significance, concluding his analysis of the *anomie* generated by incoherent values with the statements: "Suicide varies inversely with the degree of integration of religious society. Suicide varies inversely with the degree of integration of domestic society. Suicide varies inversely with the degree of integration of political society."[4] If the matter were only that simple, suicide statistics would meet most of our needs. As we have seen, however, the personality system and the social system do not coincide exactly; and suicide is a particularistic, personal response to pressures on an individual personality — not a universalistic, impersonal attack on a particular status or category (such as the killing of *any* rich man). Moreover, the propensity to make the self an object of aggression is not evenly distributed among societies or throughout a particular society; it is a culturally-specific behavioral trait, and within a system, it occurs more often among high-status, fully-socialized individuals than among the occupants of lower statuses.

Psychoanalytically speaking, "Suicide is . . . a function of an excessively strict and punishing 'superego' or internalized restraining mechanism of the personality which prohibits the outward expression of aggression."[5] This powerful superego is thought to be most pronounced in high-status personalities — that is, in those individuals who have been most thoroughly socialized into and are most positively oriented toward a culture's dominant ethical principles and norms. The high-status occupant's greater understanding of the network of privileges and obligations which gives coherence to social life makes it more difficult for him to adopt external sociopolitical targets for his aggression. It has also been argued that differences in the behavioral restraints placed on low-status and high-status individuals account for the difference in the two groups' respective suicide rates. For example, A. L. Wood has argued that low-status persons "feel oppression from others and/or the overbearing sanctions of social norms, thereby finding it psychologically expedient to blame others for their frustrations. High status persons experience less external restraint, and finding it difficult to hold others responsible for their frustrations, they turn aggression inward upon themselves."[6]

Even if we accept these tentative explanations of high-status suicide, we are a long way from being able to say that aggression against the self represents a Socrates-like reaction to systemic disequilibrium. Suicide is the act of a disoriented personality, and this disorientation may be the result of congenital malformation of the mazeway, atypical life experiences (including ill health), or the tensions produced by a social system's disequilibrium. Some amount of suicide exists in all functional societies, and it is, therefore, only marked increases in the rate of suicide that could indicate a rising degree of disequilibrium. Moreover, since suicide is a function of a particular value structure and of the needs of an individual personality socialized in accordance with it, "normal" levels of suicide and the criteria governing marked increases in the rates of suicides will differ among cultures. Suicide can therefore be considered a personal, antisocial response to systemic disequilibrium only after careful study of the suicide rates within a given society over a long period of time.

Gross suicide rates do correlate with known periods of value-environmental dissynchronization in various societies. South Africa, for example, has had a steadily rising suicide rate among both white and Negro populations as the society's integration has come to rest increasingly on armed force (see Table 6-1; Negro rates have been compiled only since 1956). Rates for whites are three times greater than for Negroes, corresponding to the general principle that suicide is the response of disoriented persons strongly committed to a system's values. Nevertheless, the trend is upward for both races, suggesting that a significant number of these suicides were motivated by a desire to reduce the tensions of societal

Table 6-1   SUICIDE, SOUTH AFRICA, 1951–1960

Year	White		Negro	
	Number	Rate/100,000	Number	Rate/100,000
1951	267	10.1	—	—
1952	252	9.4	—	—
1953	328	11.9	—	—
1954	310	11.1	—	—
1955	—	11.3	—	—
1956	322	11.1	38	3.0
1957	339	11.5	37	2.8
1958	374	12.4	42	3.1
1959	367	12.0	43	3.1
1960	437	14.2	65	4.3

Source: World Health Organization, Division of Health Statistics, *Annual Epidemiological and Vital Statistics*, Part I, Vital Statistics and Causes of Death, "Death by Cause According to Age and Sex. South Africa." Annual.

Table 6-2   SUICIDE, FRANCE, 1945–1960

Year	Number	Rate/1,000,000
1945	—	124
1946	—	119
1947	—	130
1948	—	143
1949	—	152
1950	6402	153
1951	6567	155
1952	6547	154
1953	6568	153
1954	6974	163
1955	6903	159
1956	7577	174
1957	7268	165
1958	7391	166
1959	7571	168
1960	7223	—

Source: Institut National de la Statistique et des Etudes Economiques, *Annuaire Statistique de la France.* Paris: Imprimerie Nationale. Rates taken from 1960 *retrospectif* edition; numbers from annual editions.

disequilibrium. Similarly, in France between 1945 and 1960, suicide rates correlate with the crisis of the Fourth Republic and show a slight decline after President de Gaulle restored a degree of confidence in the ability of the system to change nonviolently (see Table 6-2).

It is easy to pick out the Great Depression in America from United States' suicide statistics. The year 1932 produced the highest nationwide suicide rate between 1910 and 1958 (see Table 6-3), and the figures for the various states are even more revealing. The Connecticut suicide rate in 1932, 20.6 per 100,000, was the highest since 1909 (21.1), as compared with rates of 12.6 in 1925 and 9.7 in 1960. The 1932 rates of 15.1 per 100,000 of population in Massachusetts and 21.0 per 100,000 in New York are the highest ever recorded in these states between 1900 and 1960.[7] If we regard the depression as a major period of value-environmental dissynchronization — one in which revolution was avoided only by

Table 6-3   SUICIDE, UNITED STATES, 1910–1958

Year	Rate/100,000	Year	Rate/100,000	Year	Rate/100,000
1910	15.3	1926	12.6	1943	10.2
1911	16.0	1927	13.2	1944	10.0
1912	15.6	1928	13.5	1945	11.2
1913	15.4	1929	13.9	1946	11.5
1914	16.1	1930	15.6	1947	11.5
1915	16.2	1931	16.8	1948	11.2
1916	13.7	1932	17.4	1949	11.4
1917	13.0	1933	15.9	1950	11.4
1918	12.3	1934	14.9	1951	10.4
1919	11.5	1935	14.3	1952	10.0
1920	10.2	1936	14.3	1953	10.1
1921	12.4	1937	15.0	1954	10.1
1922	11.7	1938	15.3	1955	10.2
1923	11.5	1939	14.1	1956	10.0
1924	11.9	1940	14.4	1957	9.8
1925	12.0	1941	12.9	1958	10.2
		1942	12.0		

Source: U.S. Department of Health, Education, and Welfare; Public Health Service, *Vital Statistics of the United States* (Washington: Government Printing Office, 1900–1958).

a drastic program of reform to restore confidence in the system — we might conclude that in the United States a suicide rate above 17 per 100,000 of population signifies that a certain number of suicides are being caused by disequilibrium-induced tensions.*

Suicide statistics, however, can never do more than contribute to an index of disequilibrium. Since suicide is by its very nature a personal, particularistic response to a crisis occurring within an individual personality system, we can use it only as a crude indicator of social systemic conditions. As we have repeatedly observed, the personality and social systems are partially complementary, but each may vary greatly without influencing the other. To use suicide statistics as the sole measure of a social system's degree of equilibrium would be to commit the error of psychological reductionism.

Another indicator of dissynchronization, one that derives directly from social systems theory, is the increased production and acceptance of ideological constructs for rationalizing personal tensions. Unfortunately, it is very difficult to construct an indicator of ideological activity. The degree and nature of police intelligence work, the numbers of political associations, and sectarian and schismatic activity among religious groups might all contribute to an index of disequilibrium. Another *potential* indicator is the sales and circulation figures for ideological newspapers and journals. Table 6-4, for example, reveals a marked correlation between high circulation figures for an American fundamentalist, patriotic magazine and the depression years of 1932 and 1933. There are, of course, many difficulties connected with attempting to use this last indicator. How is an "ideological journal" to be

---

* John K. Galbraith points out that it is a popular myth that the stock market crash of 1929 produced an epidemic of suicides. The rate for October and November 1929 was, in fact, lower than for the summer months, when the stock market was still booming. However, Galbraith acknowledges that suicides rose to their highest levels during 1931 and 1932, "years when there were many things besides the stock market to cause people to conclude that life was no longer worth living." *The Great Crash, 1929* (Boston: Houghton Mifflin Sentry Editions, paperbound ed., 1954), p. 133. This pattern seems to illustrate the principle that internal tension-managing mechanisms of the personality cause delays in behavioral responses to the pressures of increasing systemic disequilibrium.

defined? How can accurate statistics on circulation be obtained (e.g., on the U.S. Communist Party's *Daily Worker*)? More seriously, since most ideological journals do not remain in publication for a long period of time, how are we to use their circulation figures as a measure of growing dissynchronization? Despite such problems, the collection and correlation of these figures might offer partial insights into the level of ideological activity in a particular social system.

Table 6-4 CIRCULATION FIGURES, AMERICAN LEGION MAGAZINE, 1921–1945

Year	Circulation	Year	Circulation
1921	778,341	1934	847,027
1922	757,237	1935	762,380
1923	708,620	1936	853,249
1924	711,511	1937	858,184
1925	660,456	1938	956,545
1926	657,006	1939	916,486
1927	647,744	1940	963,286
1928	676,601	1941	993,320
1929	703,350	1942	1,020,513
1930	756,378	1943	1,046,414
1931	830,680	1944	1,035,968
1932	939,125	1945	1,234,630
1933	1,032,960		

Source: N. W. Ayer & Son, *Directory of Newspapers and Periodicals* (Philadelphia: N. W. Ayer & Son, 1921–1945).

An extremely complex but very important indicator of increasing disequilibrium is the so-called "military participation ratio." Andrzejewski originally conceived it as a measurement of the extent to which a system's armed forces were drawn from either an exclusive military caste or the general population. Here we use it simply to mean the ratio between uniformed armed forces and the total population. The relevance of this ratio to systemic functioning derives from the differential demands made on a system's legitimate means of force, depending on the equilibrium of the social system. When a power deflation occurs and the system's integration rests increasingly on compulsion, the elite has a greater need for, and hence must expand, the system's armed police. Thus, growing numbers of police in relation to the size of a population suggest, *ceteris paribus*, that the trust generated by value sharing is being eroded and that armed force is being used to maintain a system's integration.

Such an indicator can, of course, be only a partial index of disequilibrium. In wartime the military participation ratio rises to its highest levels without necessarily being a measure of intra-systemic instability. More problematical, a rising military participation ratio is a sign of both systemic disequilibrium and the determination of the elite to maintain its authority. In situations where all other measures of instability *except* the military participation ratio are rising, there is an even greater likelihood that dissynchronized conditions will result in revolution. The elite that makes no effort to defend its authority when under attack is very likely to lose its authority by inviting a revolution. The military participation ratio thus can also be used as a crude measure of a system's counterrevolutionary potential.

Again taking the depression era in the United States as a typical example of a disequilibrated period, we find that the size of the National Guard grew during the early years of 1930–32, prior to the onset of serious elite efforts to restore equilibrium (see Table 6-5). The National Guard (the state militia prior to June 3, 1916) is the logical force for portraying the American military participation ratio since it is more often used to suppress internal insurrection than the regular army. Although the regular army also fluctuated in size during the period 1919 to 1941, its variations were in response to many political forces other than potential domestic resorts to violence.

Comparable fluctuations in the military participation ratio can also be seen by looking at the sizes of uniformed police forces in various large American cities.* During the period 1922 to 1947, for example, New York City had its largest numbers of policemen

---

* Tables 6-5, 6-6 and 6-7 should be correlated with population fluctuations in order to produce an accurate military participation ratio. The present use of absolute numbers is intended only to illustrate how the concept of the military participation ratio might be applied.

Measuring disequilibrium

Table 6-5 MILITARY PARTICIPATION RATIO, UNITED STATES,
1919–1941

Year	Regular Army Total	National Guard Total	Officers	Enlisted Men
1919	836,882	37,210	1,198	36,012
1920	200,367	56,090	2,073	54,017
1921	227,374	113,640	5,843	107,797
1922	146,069	159,658	8,744	150,914
1923	130,964	160,598	9,675	150,923
1924	140,644	177,428	10,996	166,432
1925	134,624	177,525	11,595	165,930
1926	133,033	174,969	11,435	163,534
1927	133,079	181,142	12,192	168,950
1928	134,331	181,221	12,428	168,793
1929	137,360	176,988	12,535	164,453
1930	137,472	182,715	12,930	169,785
1931	138,648	187,386	13,249	174,137
1932	133,042	187,412	13,549	173,863
1933	135,011	185,925	13,569	172,356
1934	136,970	184,791	13,507	171,284
1935	137,960	185,915	13,571	172,344
1936	166,114	189,173	13,721	175,452
1937	178,101	192,161	14,110	178,051
1938	183,447	197,188	14,443	182,745
1939	187,886	199,491	14,666	184,825
1940	264,035	241,612	14,775	226,837
1941	870,261	452,850	21,274	431,576

Source: U.S. Bureau of the Census, *Statistical Abstract of the United States*
(Washington: Government Printing Office, 1949), p. 225.

in the years 1931, 1932, and 1933 (Table 6-6). One of the many
problems with police manpower figures is that they are also influenced by many factors other than the need for police services. For
example, there is a drop in uniformed police during World War
II as a result of the reduced availability of qualified men (see
Tables 6-6 and 6-7). Yet in June of 1943, Detroit was the scene of
one of America's worst race riots. This riot, however, may be an
instance of a disequilibrated situation exacerbated by the failure of
the military participation ratio to rise. Shogan and Craig, in their
study of the Detroit riot, concluded that what began as a few hot-

Table 6-6 UNIFORMED POLICE, NEW YORK CITY, 1922–1947

Year	Number of Police	Year	Number of Police
1922	11,837	1935	17,842
1923	12,619	1936	18,045
1924	13,109	1937	18,358
1925	14,216	1938	18,645
1926	15,853	1939	18,360
1927	16,801	1940	18,177
1928	17,577	1941	17,926
1929	17,710	1942	17,582
1930	18,595	1943	17,210
1931	19,315	1944	15,579
1932	19,275	1945	15,068
1933	18,923	1946	16,973
1934	18,268	1947	17,492

Source: Police Department, City of New York, *Annual Report,* 1920–1947.

Table 6-7 UNIFORMED POLICE, DETROIT, 1928–1949

Year	Number of Police	Year	Number of Police
1928	3274	1939	3674
1929	3687	1940	3629
1930	—	1941	3665
1931	3766	1942	3528
1932	3543	1943	3474
1933	3541	1944	3395
1934	3570	1945	3488
1935	3571	1946	3690
1936	3583	1947	4123
1937	3824	1948	4205
1938	3765	1949	4373

Source: Police Department, City of Detroit, *Annual Report,* 1928–1950.

weather skirmishes developed into a full-blown rebellion chiefly because the rioters became convinced that no retaliation against their actions was in the offing. Federal Army troops eventually had to be used to restore order.[8]

When a rising military participation ratio cannot be explained in terms of one of the many external factors that may cause an elite to build up an army, it is one of the surest signs that a system is experiencing a power deflation. The South African system has been relatively free from international demands on its police services; yet it shows a marked increase in the military participation ratio beginning in 1948, the year that the intransigent policies of *apartheid* went into effect. Although the military participation ratio fell slightly between 1949 and 1957, it remained at levels higher than any previously recorded, and in 1958 it reached its all-

Table 6-8 CRIME AND POLICE, SOUTH AFRICA, 1912–1961

Year	Police per 1,000	Prosecutions per 1,000	Year	Police per 1,000	Prosecutions per 1,000
1912	1.42	46	1937	1.12	77
1913	0.94	45	1938	1.11	79
1914	0.99	42	1939	1.10	82
1915	1.23	44	1940	1.08	80
1916	1.22	47	1941	1.06	76
1917	1.23	44	1942	1.03	71
1918	1.14	40	1943	1.02	75
1919	1.22	45	1944	1.01	77
1920	1.53	47	1945	1.14	76
1921	1.52	48	1946	1.31	86
1922	1.44	49	1947	1.55	89
1923	1.42	54	1948	1.73	92
1924	1.40	57	1949	1.58	96
1925	1.36	57	1950	1.50	92
1926	1.35	61	1951	1.47	96
1927	1.35	65	1952	1.54	99
1928	1.33	66	1953	1.67	105
1929	1.31	67	1954	1.63	112
1930	1.31	71	1955	1.63	117
1931	1.32	72	1956	1.61	119
1932	1.19	72	1957	1.58	113
1933	1.19	74	1958	1.90	115
1934	1.19	76	1959	1.82	118
1935	1.20	80	1960	1.70	101
1936	1.12	74	1961	1.67	100

Source: *Annual Report of the Commissioner of the South African Police for the Year 1962* (Pretoria: The Government Printer, 1964), Annexure E.

time high of 1.90 per 1,000 population. Only the years 1920 and 1921 offer figures of an even comparable magnitude (see Table 6-8).

Together with an increase in the number of police relative to the size of a population, we would expect to find an increase in the number of times these police were actually used during periods when the system was disequilibrated. That is to say, gross crime rates, and particularly the rates for political crimes, should increase as cultural distortion develops. This is precisely the case revealed by South African criminal statistics, which show a progressively greater number of "serious crimes" each year from 1947 to 1956 (see Table 6-9). The increase of 55 percent in

Table 6-9 SERIOUS CRIME, SOUTH AFRICA, 1947–1956

Year	Number of Cases Reported	Increase over Previous Year	
		Number	Per cent
1947	84,651	9,335	11.02%
1948	89,130	4,479	5.29%
1949	138,272	49,142	55.14%
1950	148,786	10,514	7.60%
1951	158,513	9,727	6.54%
1952	167,878	9,365	5.91%
1953	169,153	1,275	0.76%
1954	183,424	14,271	8.44%
1955	193,986	10,562	5.76%
1956	215,826	21,840	11.26%

Source: C. I. Rademeyer, Commissioner of the South African Police, *Annual Report for the Year 1956* (Pretoria: The Government Printer, 1958), p. 5.

1949 was due to a reclassification of certain offenses, previously regarded as non-serious, in accordance with the revised criminal code of January 1, 1949 — viz., crimes against the state (*Crimen Laesae Majestatis*), instigating racial hostility between Europeans and non-Europeans, and resisting or obstructing the police. The reclassification of these crimes was itself a sign of growing systemic disequilibrium; the system's integration was tending toward a basis in institutionalized norms rather than in common values.

Prewar Germany also provides some interesting correlations between the crime rate and disequilibrated social conditions. Gross criminal statistics between 1914 and 1940 clearly pinpoint the revolutionary year of 1923, but they also indicate that the conditions of disequilibrium prevailing in that year were only partially relieved during the succeeding decade (see Table 6-10). Not until 1933 did the numbers of convicted murderers and felons begin to decline significantly, a fact presumably explained by the social changes promised and initiated by the Nazis. However, this conclusion can only be drawn with the help of hindsight. The total number of convictions in each year between 1924 and 1932 is actually smaller than the figure for 1923, so that it is equally possible to argue that social conditions were improving prior to the rise of Hitler. Some criteria for what constituted a significant change in the crime rate would have to be established in order to use these figures as part of an overall index of systemic disequilibrium.

It is an unavoidable conclusion that the statistics offered in this chapter cannot be taken as truly adequate signs of disequilibrated social systems. Suicide, crime, the military participation ratio, and other individual symptoms of social disequilibrium are all influenced by numerous factors other than the value structure's coherence with the division of labor. Even if the rates we have discussed could be taken as reliable indicators of systemic disequilibrium, the statistics we have been using were collected for purposes other than measuring a system's stability and are therefore open to question. Indicators of disequilibrium which were not discussed here, such as a system's greater reliance on formal norms in lieu of agreement on values, the breakdown in definitions of crime and lunacy, the polarization of a society into manifest interest groups, and incoherence in the processes of socialization, would all require novel and experimental statistical techniques to reduce them to measurable quantities. I do not possess the skills necessary for this task, and I retain a deeply ingrained suspicion of facile attempts to make statements about whole societies on the basis of one or two variables.

Nevertheless, it would seem that an index of systemic instability, comparable to the various indices of economic trends, could be constructed and that such an index would be of great

CRIME, GERMANY, 1914-1940

Year	Indictments	Acquittals	Numbers Sentenced			
			Total	Men	Women	Juveniles
1914	560,024	97,047	454,064	376,194	77,870	46,940
1915	349,308	57,191	287,535	212,135	75,400	63,126
1916	350,400	58,348	287,500	201,100	86,400	80,399
1917	357,146	58,269	294,584	191,778	102,806	95,651
1918	408,147	61,447	341,526	213,603	127,923	99,498
1919	418,064	61,643	348,247	262,793	85,454	64,619
1920	733,458	115,152	608,563	489,814	118,749	91,171
1921	797,552	135,206	651,148	520,598	130,550	76,932
1922	760,706	113,955	636,817	522,933	113,884	72,124
1923	968,883	133,995	823,902	688,959	134,943	86,040
1924	827,021	118,342	696,668	582,180	114,488	43,276
1925	682,092	94,691	575,745	482,378	93,367	24,771
1926	700,201	98,728	589,611	500,267	89,344	24,066
1927	724,258	102,915	608,356	516,366	91,990	24,119
1928	691,710	93,468	585,862	502,405	83,457	27,104
1929	704,247	96,594	593,707	512,127	81,580	25,673
1930	708,847	99,345	594,610	515,260	79,350	26,409
1931	685,355	103,423	564,903	492,530	72,373	22,844
1932	691,921	104,106	564,479	500,993	63,486	21,529
1933	590,165	75,933	489,090	430,917	58,173	15,958
1934	460,269	58,260	383,885	329,688	54,197	12,294
1935	499,955	55,588	429,355	368,112	61,243	17,028
1936	440,530	46,471	383,315	328,391	54,924	16,855
1937	504,093	54,032	438,493	370,458	68,035	24,562
1938	381,817	38,350	335,665	282,510	53,155	19,302
1939	335,162	31,038	297,353	251,043	46,310	17,444
1940	292,039	21,270	264,625	205,141	59,484	21,274

Source: Derived from Statistiches Reichsamt, *Statistisches Jahrbuch für das Deutsche Reich* (Berlin, 1941-42 ed.), p. 649.

value both in testing particular propositions in social systems theory and in heading off the destructiveness of revolutionary change. If and when social scientists agree upon some model of the social system as their conceptual paradigm, the construction of such indices is likely to become the main task of routine social science. Until that time, statistical indicators of disequilibrium should be employed with great circumspection.

7

Varieties
of revolution

On the evening of July 14, 1789, the Duc de Rochefoucauld-Liancourt told King Louis XVI of the fall of the Bastile, to which the King responded, "Mais, c'est une révolte!" "Non, sire," the Duke corrected him, "ce n'est pas une révolte, c'est une révolution." In so doing he gave classic expression to the now universal distinction between "rebellion" and "revolution." Writing in 1854, Thomas Meadows perpetuated this old contrast in his often repeated observation that the Chinese were (then) the most rebellious and the least revolutionary people on earth. The problem with both Liancourt and Meadows is that there has always been a great deal of confusion as to what they were distinguishing: today we call Fidel Castro's seizure of power the Cuban "revolution," but we refer to the massive peasant war of nineteenth-century China as the Taiping "rebellion," and we call the Budapest insurrection of 1956 either the Hungarian Rebellion or the Hungarian Revolution. Further confounding the picture, we refer to some other famous instances of political violence as the Indian "Mutiny," the Paris "Commune," the American "Civil

War," and the Kapp "Putsch" — all of which involved insurrectionary resorts to arms.

Amid this tradition of imprecision, several scholars continue to write prefaces in which they declare their interest is in "great revolutions" and that they intend to eschew the study of "mere rebellions," but without ever telling us how they propose to differentiate between the two. Our earlier explanation of the causes of any insurrection in terms of power deflation, loss of authority, and the intervention of an accelerator applies equally to what are here distinguished as "revolutions" and "rebellions." However, this earlier analysis did not touch on why resorts to political violence take different forms. This is an extremely complex problem, but one way to begin to penetrate it is by sharpening the traditional distinction between rebellion and revolution.

"Medieval and post-medieval theory," writes Hannah Arendt, "knew of legitimate rebellion, of rise against established authority, of open defiance and disobedience. But the aim of such rebellions was not a challenge of authority or the established order of things as such; it was always a matter of exchanging the person who happened to be in authority, be it the exchange of a usurper for the legitimate king or the exchange of a tyrant who had abused his power for a lawful ruler."[1] Here is the simplest and clearest meaning of rebellion. Political principles inform the actions of the rebels, but the rebellion is not caused by a dispute over principles. The rebels know how the society ought to be governed — namely, in the way they remember its being governed before the usurper or tyrant betrayed the trust that the society had placed in him. Rebellion in this sense is an act of social surgery; it is intended to cut out one or more members who are offending against the joint commitments to maintain a particular social structure. Locke used the term rebellion in precisely this sense; in fact, he thought that it was the tyrant who rebelled and that the act of deposing him was no rebellion. Simple rebellion, we may say, is without ideology; its ideology is actually a functioning structure of values which informs the people that one or more of their authority statuses is actually occupied by a usurper or a tyrant.

The classic example of a simple rebellion is a jacquerie. Both the historic Jacquerie (1358) and subsequent rebellions similar to it were motivated by a belief that the system had been betrayed by its elite; violence was invoked in order to purge the system of its violators and, so to speak, to set it back on the tracks. Masses rebelling in order to restore an *ancien régime*, or one patterned after it, are not alienated from the description of reality contained in the old value structure. Jacqueries have usually been carried out in the name of a king or church, against the allegedly unworthy local agents of that king or church, or against agents of a foreign king or church. E. I. Pugachev, for example, the leader of the large-scale Russian peasant rebellion of 1773–75, exploited the popular belief that Peter III had not been murdered and declared that he was rebelling in the name of the rightful Tsar. He united behind this banner peasants, cossacks, runaway serfs, and Tartar bands — all of whom were rebelling against the progressive curtailment of the rights of the lower strata during the eighteenth century.

Concerning jacquerie ideology, Hobsbawm has written: "The peasants did not rise for the real king, whom they hardly knew, but for the ideal of the just king who, if he only knew, would punish the transgressions of his underlings and lords; though often they did rise for the real church. For the village priest was one of them, the saints were certainly theirs and nobody else's, and even the tumbledown ecclesiastical estates were sometimes more tolerable than the grasping laymen."[2] Potential jacquerie conditions may persist for a long time until some occurrence — such as humiliation by a foreign power, or open banditry, or another rebellion elsewhere in the realm — reveals that the existing elites are incapable of performing their roles. The typical remedy for these conditions will be a purge of the elites by the masses.

Generally speaking, simple rebellions are not motivated by an *ideology*; the goal culture of such a movement is actually a fully elaborated structure of values that the rebels believe is still capable of organizing their communal life. A recent example is the Tibetan Rebellion of 1959. There are, however, other forms of rebellion which espouse the revival or reintroduction of an idealized society that allegedly existed in the society's own past. These movements advocate the creation of a pattern of social organization which the rebels justify by a claim to traditional legitimacy, although they may actually break with tradition in many of the institutions that they seek to establish. Examples include the counterrevolution in the Vendée in 1793, the ideology of the Confederate rebels in the American Civil War, the nostalgia of the Puritans for a pre-Norman England, and the ideology of the Franco forces in the Spanish Civil War. In describing these revolts we shall continue to use the term "rebellion," although it is clear that they involve changes of a greater magnitude than the removal of offending personnel.

The historical European Anarchist movement offers us an example of the ideology encountered in the more advanced type of rebellion. As Woodcock has observed, "It [Anarchism] was a protest, a dedicated resistance to the worldwide trend since the middle of the eighteenth century toward political and economic centralization, with all it implies in terms of the replacement of personal values by collective values, of the subordination of the individual to the state. . . . They [the Anarchists] drew their support mainly from those social classes which were out of tune with the dominant historical trend and which were steadily declining in numbers."[3] The Anarchists articulated goals for the future that derived from an idealized but increasingly redundant past. They hoped to escape from the tensions generated by rapid social change by restoring a simpler, pre-national, pre-industrial life which placed greater reliance on cooperation than on authority. Anarchist rebellions were, in this sense, restorative rather than revolutionary.

When the goal culture of an insurrectionary ideology envisions the recasting of the social division of labor according to a pattern which is self-consciously unprecedented in the context of a particular social system, then we should use the term "revolution." Revolutions of course also involve attacks upon certain persons; all insurrections have that as a goal. But revolution intends to accomplish more. It is distinguished from its nearest rival, the ideological rebellion, by its conscious espousal of a new social order, be it a society based on "The Rights of Man and Citizen," the ideal of "self-determination," or the principle of "from each according to his ability, to each according to his needs."

As the distinction between simple and ideological rebellions was necessary, so there is a need to distinguish simple and total revolutions. Some revolutionary ideologies are restricted to fundamental changes in only a few values — for example, values governing access to the statuses of authority, or economic exchange, or the resolution of conflicting goals — but such revolutions do not contemplate alterations in the values controlling religious beliefs, basic political identity, or sex- and age-based status differentials. In some cases, the goals of simple revolutions can be achieved through promulgating or rewriting a political constitution for the system, as in the case of General de Gaulle's seizure of power in 1958 or, to a large extent, in the American Revolution. Of course, the implementation of demands for revolutionary changes in certain values may give rise over time to either homeostatic or deliberate reinterpretations of most of the other values in a system in order to maintain a coherent and integrated social structure. But changes subsequent to, and arising as a consequence of, revolutionary change need not themselves be of the revolutionary variety. On the other hand, a simple revolution intended to resolve certain dissynchronized conditions may produce new conditions of disequilibrium which the elite is unable or unwilling to relieve through policies of change, thereby setting the stage for a later total revolution.

Total revolutions, such as the one in France that began in 1789 or in China throughout much of this century, aim at supplanting the entire structure of values and at recasting the entire division of labor. In France between 1789 and 1797, the people employed violence to change the systems of landholding, taxation, choice of occupation, education, prestige symbols, military organization, and virtually every other characteristic of the social system. Its effect was to transform Provençals, Bretons, Alsatians, and so forth, into Frenchmen. This is the kind of revolution which, when successful, alters the social system from one major archetype to another — e.g., from feudalism to capitalism, or from peasant community to national community. This type is, of course, extremely rare. Changes in basic political and social consciousness seldom occur at a fixed point in time (viz., the slowness of change in both white and Negro attitudes vis-à-vis the "integration" of Negroes into the American social system), and the extent to which changes of such magnitude have ever been achieved through revolution remains a controversial matter. Nevertheless, some revolutionary ideologies, such as that of Chinese communism, do envisage a total reformulation of both the value structure and the pattern of environmental adaptation of a social system. Our immediate criterion for differentiating between rebellion and revolution will therefore be, following Hannah Arendt, the aims or goal cultures of the various movements.

The differences between simple and ideological rebellions and simple and total revolutions should not, of course, be treated as dichotomies. Every revolution reveals shades of difference from all other cases, and many concrete revolutionary movements began as rebellions and turned into revolutions as they encountered difficulties in actually securing the changes demanded (e.g., the revolution of 1776 in the United States). Simple rebellion and total revolution should be understood as polar extremes along a continuum of insurrectionary variation.

The differences between rebellion and revolution may be made clearer if they are viewed in terms of the levels of sociopolitical organization upon which they impinge. The idea of "levels" of society has been formulated in many different ways in the past, but for our purposes a simple threefold distinction among the levels of *government, regime,* and *community* is sufficient.[4] By "government," we mean the formal political and administrative institutions that make and execute decisions for the society — that is to say, the institutionalized expressions of the statuses of authority. Resorts to violence in order to cause changes at this level will be simple rebellions; they seek to replace persons who are believed to be occupying various authority positions illegitimately.

"Regime" refers to the fundamental rules of the political game in a society: democracy, dictatorship, monarchy, oligarchy, federalism, constitutionalism, and the like, are characteristics of different kinds of regimes. Ideological rebellions and simple revolutions normally aim at this level — i.e., at the normative codes governing political and economic behavior, which are thought to be in need of change. Revolts which seek to establish or broaden popular suffrage, or alter the norms of land tenure, or oust foreign conquerors, are examples of attempts to change the system at the level of the regime.

By "community," we mean the broadest level of social organization and consciousness, the level where fundamental values cohere with the cardinal demands of environmental adaptation. It is here that we speak of, for example, the values of "peasant society" combined with "subsistence polyculture." If the mode of production in such a society shifts to one-crop cultivation for a market and a revolution is required to bring its values into line with this radically different pattern of environmental adaptation, the revolution will be total. Similarly, when people cease to regard themselves primarily as members of kinship or religious communities and become members of national communities, a change in basic political consciousness has taken place. If this change occurs under revolutionary auspices, the revolution will be of the magnitude of the one in France during the eighteenth century, or in China during this century.

A typology of revolutions parallel to the one being set forth, also using the concept of levels, is that of James Rosenau. He distinguishes among revolutions in terms of the "targets" of the revolutionaries, and on this basis he identifies three types (he uses the term "[internal] war" instead of revolution): personnel wars, authority wars, and structural wars.[5] His personnel wars and structural wars correspond, respectively, to our revolutions aimed at the levels of government and the community. His "authority" wars, while corresponding roughly to our revolutions aimed at the regime, are somewhat misnamed since, as we have seen earlier, *all* rebellions and revolutions involve challenges to the authority of *status quo* elites.

Still another attempt to distinguish types of revolutions using the element of ideology as the criterion of differentiation is by Anthony Wallace. The three types he suggests are: "Movements which profess to *revive* a traditional culture now fallen into desuetude; movements which profess to *import* a foreign cultural system; and movements which profess neither revival nor importation, but conceive that the desired cultural end-state, which has never been enjoyed by ancestors or foreigners, will be realized for the first time in a future *Utopia*."[6]

Wallace's first category corresponds exactly to the traditional idea of rebellion, according to which all rebellions seek to put back into perfect working order a social system that has, from the perspective of an earlier period of time, diverged from its inner logic. Similarly, Wallace's Utopian movements correspond to total revolutions, in which the revolutionaries see themselves as the instruments, or creators, of "progress" toward a newer and better form of communal life. However, these categories are a little too broad, and Wallace himself points out that, "It is easy to demonstrate that avowedly revival movements are never entirely what they claim to be, for the image of the ancient culture to be revived is distorted by historical ignorance and by the presence of imported and innovative elements."[7] This fact suggests the need to distinguish between purely revivalist movements — or simple rebellions — and rebellions that consciously develop an *ideology* of earlier social perfection. While many simple rebellions, such as some of the widespread peasant uprisings associated with changes of dynasty in traditional China, both espoused and succeeded in reestablishing a virtual mirror image of the social *status quo ante*, there are also more developed ideologies, such as those of the Boxers or the Mau Mau, which should be distinguished from the Lockean type of revolt. By the same token, some revolutions are genuinely Utopian, but many others, typically those occurring at the level of the regime, demand innovations which fall well short of reconstituting the system.

The greatest problem with Wallace's typology is his belief that the importation of ideology makes a difference. It seems highly unlikely that any successful movement ever "professed" to be the agent of a foreign cultural system; the history of international communism since the Russian Revolution alone suggests that such an avowal is tantamount to ideological suicide. Imported ideological constructs always undergo a process of domestication: what Mao Tse-tung has done for Marxism in a modern Chinese context, Hung Hsiu-ch'üan did a century earlier for Christianity in a Taiping context (he declared himself to be the younger brother of Jesus Christ). While it is true that many revolutionary ideologies gain their initial currency through culture contact, Wallace does not demonstrate how this produces a different variety of revolution. As we observed earlier, the endogenous or exogenous nature of *sources of change* is highly relevant to discovering the causes of a system's disequilibrium, but this factor does not determine that one or another kind of revolution will necessarily occur.

The distinction between rebellion and revolution provides a beginning for a typology of revolts, and its usefulness may be improved through the addition of various relevant criteria, such as the levels at which revolutionary activity is aimed. However, even when perfected, any typology of this sort runs the danger of excessive abstraction and superficiality. This is because of the contingent nature of revolution (using the word "revolution" in its generic sense rather than as one *kind* of political violence), a characteristic that has been stressed throughout this book. Revolution is a response to a particular crisis in a particular social system, and any attempt to compare revolutions that does not at the same time compare social systems is theoretically inconsistent. The fundamental factors that give rise to variation among revolutions are the types of system in which they occur and the conditions of systemic disequilibrium that they seek to overcome. These two elements must form the foundation of any serious study of a concrete case of revolution.[8]

Unfortunately, generalizing about types of social systems is still extremely difficult. In contemporary social science research, this subject is receiving the almost exclusive attention of political sociologists and students of political and economic development. In this volume we cannot hope to do more than suggest several approaches to the problem, but it should be evident from our earlier analysis that the study of types of revolutions and the study of types of social systems are inseparable. We may be able to define abstractly the different meanings of the words "rebellion" and "revolution," but we can never compare the Algerian and Vietnamese revolutions without thoroughly investigating the Algerian and Vietnamese social systems.

The best-known social scientific attempt to categorize societies is that of Marx. Basing his analysis on the alleged primacy of the pattern of environmental adaptation — or, the "modes of production" — he discovered six types of societies. These he called: primitive communism, slavery, feudalism, capitalism, socialism, and communism; and he linked them in an evolutionary chain of development. The dynamic elements that caused one type to change into the next were the dialectical generation of social classes, followed by class warfare and revolutionary change. He also discovered some types of societies that stood outside his evolutionary framework — for example, "Oriental Despotism," or the "Asiatic mode of production" — but he did nothing more than identify them as anomalies. Contemporary social scientists studying the same problems have reacted strongly against the Marxist conception — both against the idea of an evolutionary chain of development, for which the evidence is lacking, and against the use of economic criteria as the primary categorizing principles.

Parsons, for example, has perfected a widely-used set of criteria with which he attempts to distinguish social systems on the basis of their value structures. These criteria he calls the "pattern variables," or "dilemmas of orientation"; and he posits a series of five value dichotomies in terms of which each society can be placed: (1) affectivity versus affective neutrality; (2) collectivity-orientation versus self-orientation; (3) particularism versus universalism; (4) ascription versus achievement; and (5) functional diffuseness versus functional specificity.* [9] As is readily apparent, the values of affectivity, collectivity-orientation, particularism, ascription, and functional diffuseness typify types of society that are often called "traditional"; whereas affective neutrality, self-orientation, universalism, achievement, and functional specificity are traits of societies that are popularly called "modern." The Parsonian pattern variables are, to this extent, an attempt to re-

---

* These relationships may be described somewhat less succinctly as follows: (1) the saliency of public emotional ties versus the saliency of private emotional ties; (2) the primacy of group interests versus the primacy of individual interests; (3) the basing of decisions on nonscientific, ungeneralized knowledge versus the basing of decisions on allegedly scientific laws; (4) the assignment of people to statuses on the basis of who they are versus the assignment of people to statuses on the basis of what they do; and (5) a lack of role specialization versus role multiplicity and compartmentalization. For a different expansion of the Parsonian pattern variables, see Everett E. Hagen, *On the Theory of Social Change* (Homewood, Ill.: The Dorsey Press, 1962), p. 121.

fine the older sociological distinction between *Gemeinschaft* (a community characterized by face-to-face personal relationships and ascribed, or intrinsic, statuses) and *Gesellschaft* (an atomized, secularized society that assigns persons to statuses on the basis of their achievements).

Parsons does not intend, however, that his five dichotomies should constitute one overarching dichotomy — the broadest possible distinction between two societies on the basis of all five pattern variables should be conceived only as constituting the opposite poles of continuum — and he rejects the notion of a unitary evolutionary path from one pole to the other. For example, some basically traditional societies may nevertheless use achievement to assign individuals to certain statuses, as was partly the case in the classical Chinese examination system for selecting imperial officials; and many so-called modern societies retain particularistic features, such as buying done on the basis of friendship, trust, or habit, or the persistence of school and regional ties. The pattern variables thus make an advance over the old traditional-modern distinction by providing the basis for differentiating within the larger groupings.

Of all the pattern variables, the one that has probably received the greatest amount of scholarly attention and that is most relevant to the varieties of revolution is functional diffuseness versus functional specificity. In traditional societies it is very difficult to employ such concepts as "economic man" or "political man," or to make clear distinctions among the roles of father, citizen, farmer, and civic leader. Persons living in these societies do not themselves distinguish among, for example, religion, philosophy, and science, and the roles required for fulfilling the system's functional prerequisites are not characterized by internal specialization within the system's broad strata. We use the word "peasant" to refer to a whole congeries of roles and norms, whereas the word "farmer" refers specifically to the role of agricultural production. The role of farmer does not necessarily indicate anything about the other roles that a farmer may perform, whereas the role of peasant implies a whole way of life.

Although very little research has been done on the subject, there is some evidence to suggest that functionally diffuse societies are more likely to experience rebellions, whereas functionally specific societies are more likely to experience revolutions. Diffuse societies are characterized by an almost homogeneous spreading of the system's values among all its members and, due to the lack of role specialization, by a relatively low interdependence among its parts and a relatively high degree of equilibrium.[10] Because of the homogeneity and stability of values, dissynchronized conditions are more likely to produce efforts at restoration than innovation; and because of the low degree of interdependence, exogenous sources of change are likely to have only a localized impact, which the elite may isolate or erradicate through purposeful policies of action. Many so-called primitive (pre-literate) and traditional (literate but having at best a pre-Newtonian science and technology) societies have histories of rebellion but not of revolution.

The functionally specific, or differentiated, society is one in which values and the pattern of environmental adaptation demand a highly complex ensemble of roles. The sources of change that may generate these roles include the production of goods in a factory system (industrial technology), the rise of a centralized state governing a large territory, the acceptance of a religion with a professional priesthood, the control of water for irrigation and flood prevention, and the development of towns as the loci of markets or intellectual centers.[11] As a result of such changes, certain types of work become separated from kinship, religious, regional, and other relationships; and this initial separation in turn causes other major role sets to differentiate internally and from each other.

Differentiation, or "the formation of social positions specialized in different segments of [an] activity, and the subdivision of existing social positions into more specialized ones," is directly relevant to the production of *revolutionary* ideologies.[12] Differentiation generates subsystems which, in performing their particular functions, often emphasize or modify the system's values in such a way that they begin to diverge markedly from other subsystems. As Arnold Feldman has written: "Differentiation (1) increases the number of [sub-] social systems that constitute a society; (2) increases the salience of the particular system to which a norm belongs, which increases the salience of subsystem goals and values; [and] (3) increases the discontinuity between subsystems as the normative content of each is purified and decontaminated."[13] By decontamination, Feldman means the extent to which subsystem values come to be understood by members of the subsystem in terms of structural characteristics of the system and not simply as the personal preferences or anomalies of a group of people.

Functionally differentiated societies also differ from diffuse societies in that their segments are highly interdependent and their equilibrium is more fragile. Here the roles of the system are not duplicated throughout each stratum; they diverge widely both individually and in accordance with the performance of specific functional requirements. The relationship between roles and role sets is one of coordination rather than simple complementarity, and new roles specifically charged with coordinating the numerous functions must be articulated. Because of this high degree of interdependence, and the ease with which differences over the meanings and priorities of values may arise, if the system's values become dissynchronized with its division of labor, an ideology proposing revolutionary changes in either the values or the division of labor is likely to develop. Rebellion presupposes a fair degree of agreement among people on how the society should be organized. Revolution is a manifestation of basic disagreements among many sectors of the society on precisely this point; the revolution is often an attempt to settle these disagreements by force in favor of one or another position.

The effects of differentiation are, of course, offset by patterns of multiple role playing, which will normally cause differences in value saliency to cancel each other out in the minds of individual actors. Moreover, the differentiated society will itself develop values and norms for the toleration of differences, for the peaceful resolution of conflicts, and for the routinized settlement of differences arising from value saliency as an element of maintaining a homeostatic equilibrium in a complex division of labor. However, if the preconditions for violent social change arise in such a system, the system's very complexity is more likely to suggest the need for revolutionary rather than rebellious action.

Probably for this reason Hannah Arendt noted the modernity of the concept of revolution; although the idea is not restricted to highly complex societies, it is considerably more relevant to them.

Parsons's pattern variables constitute only one of many attempts to create a typology of societies. On the basis of responses to questionnaires about political attitudes, Almond and Verba have developed a different, threefold typology of "political cultures": parochial, subject, and participant cultures. Although their theory is not specifically coordinated with other approaches to the problem of categorizing societies, their findings obviously correlate with earlier distinctions among traditional, transitional, and modern societies, and the traditional side of the pattern variables can clearly be applied to parochial cultures while the modern half relates to participant cultures. In addition to identifying these three types of cultures, Almond and Verba suggest an intersecting typology based on the degree to which people regard their respective cultures as "appropriate or satisfactory." When the parochial, subject, or participant culture is fully satisfactory, a member's orientation is said to be "allegiant"; when it is quite unsatisfactory, a member is called "alienate"; and when the system is in "transition," Almond and Verba refer to a member's attitudes as "aspirational."[14]

These are very interesting ideas. Presumably the allegiant and alienated orientations could be correlated with extreme degrees of synchronization and dissynchronization. The authors have not done so, but the attempt to work out such correlations could be an avenue of future research on political violence. The obvious drawback to this type of research is that revolution is a form of action, whereas attitudes are a notoriously treacherous guide to what people actually do. Even projective tests of orientations more subtle than attitudes are open to challenge on this score. Direct behavioral observation is a sounder indicator of systemic equilibrium than the measurement of attitudes by means of questionnaires. Equally important, from a macro-systemic perspective, is the need to distinguish theoretically between deviant alienates in an otherwise equilibrated system and political alienates in a disequilibrated system.

The typologies of Parsons and of Almond and Verba illustrate some of the more advanced attempts in contemporary social science to conceptualize the differences among social systems. The Parsonian construction is more in harmony with the orientation of the present book than that of Almond and Verba, but even it is not completely satisfactory. As we have argued earlier, the ultimate determinant of social structure is the interrelationship between a particular structure of values and the demands of adaptation in a particular sociopolitical environment. A typology of social structures must be informed by the multiple variables that go to make up this subtle relationship. Such a typology does not exist, and it would constitute more than a digression to attempt to create one here.

Lacking firm agreement on the types of social systems and, more narrowly, on the varieties of disequilibrated conditions that may arise in them, we must retreat from any claim to exhaustive study of the types of revolutions. Revolutions are determined by an extremely numerous set of variables; and, given the present state of social science theory, it is virtually impossible to isolate and recombine all of these variables into various abstract models. A more satisfactory "middle range" approach is the attempt to categorize differences among a few salient variables. We did this earlier in terms of the goal culture components of revolutionary ideologies. The renovation versus innovation distinction — or, more simply, the distinction between rebellion and revolution — remains the most widely used classification in studies of political violence. It must be reiterated, however, that none of the forms of the rebellion-revolution distinction is the equivalent of a true typology based on social systems principles.

8

Strategies
of revolution

Whereas the distinction between rebellion and revolution rests on differences in the ideologies of various movements, another time-honored way of classifying revolutions is by the different tactics of violence adopted by the revolutionaries. Thus we describe the Bolshevik Revolution as a coup d'état, the Russian revolution of 1905 as a spontaneous popular insurrection, and the Chinese and Algerian revolutions as guerrilla wars. Moreover, we attempt to create subclasses among major categories of insurrectionary tactics, speaking of "regular" revolutionary wars, rural guerrilla wars, military coups d'état, urban insurrections, and so forth.

As should be apparent from the analysis that has gone before, to classify revolutions by their tactical characteristics is even more reductionist than to explain their variability by the single factor of ideology. The ideological goal cultures of revolutionaries do offer insights into the conditions of disequilibrium that have breached a system's defenses against violence; demands for land reform, for example, indicate the need to examine a society's system of land tenure. Technologies of violence, however, are much further removed from the major variables that produce differences in form. In fact, the practice of differentiating among revolutions on a tactical basis is partly responsible for the widespread confusion over the very meaning of revolution. Not all coups d'état are revolutionary, even when they "succeed" (for example, palace revolutions and military *pronunciamientos*, or *juntas*); and some guerrilla wars are actually international policies of subversion — disguised as revolution — undertaken by one social system against another. In the latter case, the labelling of such "Fifth Column" activities as "revolutions" by their sponsors is merely a conscious element of political warfare in modern international relations of conflict (e.g., several Chinese Communist-sponsored "wars of national liberation," or the U.S. Central Intelligence Agency's sponsored revolution at the Bay of Pigs in Cuba). The fact that some conspirators call themselves revolutionaries does not, from the point of view of systems theory, make them so; whether or not they are actually revolutionaries remains a matter for social science investigation.

On the other hand, some coups d'état are revolutionary; they constitute the first stage in the relief of systemic disequilibrium and the initiation of revolutionary social change (e.g., the Bolshevik seizure of power, the March on Rome, or the coup d'état of Gamal Abdel Nasser in Egypt). Similarly, guerrilla wars that are *supported* by foreign governments should be carefully distinguished from guerrilla wars that are *sponsored* by foreign governments, and it should be recognized that degrees of support and sponsorship can and do change over time, thereby altering the nature of a movement.

Non-revolutionary coups d'état and acts of international subversion disguised as revolutions (the classic example is, of course, the Nazi Party's use of persons of German descent residing in Czechoslovakia and throughout Europe) ought to be understood, from a systems theory perspective, as either endogenous or exogenous sources of change. Very often these so-called revolutions create the conditions for a subsequent true revolution. The post-World War II seizure of power by the Hungarian Communist Party, for example, was the primary source of the disequilibrated conditions that caused the Hungarian Rebellion of 1956. Similarly, the military coup d'état against President Juan Bosch of the Dominican Republic set the stage for the Santo Domingo revolution of 1965. When non-revolutionary resorts to violence fail, as they often do, they are treated as the acts of traitors or as instances of international subversion. It is therefore inconsistent to regard them as revolutions simply because their perpetrators sometimes bring to bear overwhelming force and, as a result, are said to have "won."

The element that distinguishes the acts of criminals or lunatics (e.g., Conrad's *Secret Agent*) from a revolutionary coup d'état or a mass uprising is the functional condition of the social system in which they occur. This condition can be determined independently of the success or failure of an instance of violence against a system's elite, and in our earlier discussion of measuring systemic disequilibrium, we indicated the need for, and some possible ways of, doing so. If the condition of the system is one of power deflation and a loss of authority, violent attacks against it are to be expected. Whether these attacks take the form of a coup d'état or a civil war is of secondary importance, but this is not to suggest that revolutionary tactics are wholly irrelevant to the study of revolution. Rather, we point out that basing an analysis entirely on them can be a source of conceptual confusion.

The tactics of a revolutionary outbreak can sometimes tells us a good deal about the sort of conditions that prevail in a disequilibrated system. If there is widespread agreement on the need for change and if the *status quo* elite is relatively isolated and undefended, a coup d'état is the most economical and welcome violent way of altering the system's structure. If the elite, through its possession of overwhelming armed force, is able to frustrate all demands for change, then revolution may take the form of a prolonged revolutionary war. The choice of revolutionary method will depend on what actions the revolutionaries perceive to be necessary in order to try to implement their goal culture — or, in other words, differences in tactics illustrate differences in the "transfer cultures" of revolutionary ideologies.

The transfer culture of a revolutionary ideology — that element of the ideology which tells the revolutionaries what to do and how to do it in order to usher in the new order — in some cases dictates what will be the sufficient cause, or accelerator, of a revolution. The remote causes of a revolution — power deflation and a loss of authority — may exist without a revolution occurring, in which case the integration of a system will rest on the elite's monopoly of armed force — on the prevention of revolutionaries from organizing and on the maintenance of role performances through deterrence. In these circumstances the final cause of a revolutionary resort to arms is some event, called an "accelerator," that holds forth the promise to the revolutionaries that they can break the elite's monopoly of force. This accelerator may be some factor beyond the control of the revolutionaries, such as the crippling of the armed forces through a defeat in war, a mutiny, or dissension within elite circles; or it may be (1) an ideological belief according to which the forces of a *status quo* elite can be incapacitated through direct action against them — for example, beliefs in the intervention of supernatural powers, or in foreign assistance if the revolutionaries display determination, or in the invincibility of a mob — or (2) the launching of a strategy of revolution designed to defeat the armed forces of an entrenched elite.

The distinction among these accelerators is analytical rather than empirical. The internal dissolution of the armed forces may accompany either one of the other two accelerators; for example, the strategy of a revolutionary coup d'état often involves exploiting or exacerbating an elite's temporary loss of its armed strength before it can be reconsolidated. Similarly, both ideological and strategic accelerators are parts of "transfer cultures." The differences between them lie in the fact that the latter is amenable to strategic analysis. According to the widely accepted view of Thomas Schelling, "Among diverse theories of conflict — corresponding to the diverse meanings of the word 'conflict' — a main dividing line is between those that treat conflict as a pathological state and seek its causes and treatment, and those that take conflict for granted and study the behavior associated with it. Among the latter there is a further division between those that examine the participants in a conflict in all their complexity — with regard to both 'rational' and 'irrational' behavior, conscious and unconscious, and to motivations as well as calculations — and those that focus on the more rational, conscious, artful kind of behavior. Crudely speaking, the latter treat conflict as a kind of contest, in which the participants are trying to 'win.' A study of conscious, intelligent, sophisticated conflict behavior — of successful behavior — is like a search for rules of 'correct' behavior in a contest-winning sense. We can call this field of study the *strategy* of conflict." [1]

Strategic accelerators differ from ideological accelerators in their degree of rationality. To this it might be replied that what is "ideology" to one party may be "strategy" to another. It seems unnecessary here to digress into an extended discussion of what constitutes rationality. By the rational quality of strategy, we mean merely that *both* sides to a conflict recognize particular courses of behavior as promoting or detracting from the mutually pursued goal of victory and that one side's behavior is modified in response to the behavior of its opponent — as in the strategy of an endgame in chess. Ideological accelerators, on the other hand — such as the belief that certain initiation rites endow one with supernatural powers — are not rational in this sense; they are the products of wishful thinking, risk taking, recklessness, emotional frenzy, and so forth.

A strategy of revolution derives from a rational calculation of the forces that the *status quo* elite has mobilized against the possibility of revolution, and it elaborates courses of action intended to disarm this military preparedness. Clearly, strategies of revolution demand leadership, organization, and communications among the revolutionaries. When implemented, a strategy may or may not succeed, but both sides of the struggle take each other's actions seriously. Success or failure depends upon numerous variables which both parties will have tried to calculate, including the military variables of morale, competence of command, training, equipment, intelligence information, and so forth.

Not all revolutions are accelerated by strategies, nor are all revolutions organized, led, or informed by a supervisory directorate. Probably the simplest kind of accelerator is the "incident," which reveals to the mob that the armed forces arrayed against it have been incapacitated or which causes the mob to believe that its combined strength can overcome the armed police. Schelling comments on the differences between strategic and non-strategic, or "mob," action as follows: "It is usually the essence of mob formation that the potential members have to know not only where and when to meet but just when to act so that they act in concert. Overt leadership solves the problem; but leadership can often be identified and eliminated by the authority trying to prevent mob action. In this case the mob's problem is to act in unison without overt leadership, to find some common symbol that makes everyone confident that if he acts on it, he will not be acting alone. The role of 'incidents' can thus be seen as a coordinating role; it is a substitute for overt leadership and communication. Without something like an incident, it may be difficult to get action at all, since immunity requires that all know when to act together."[2] By contrast, the actual moment of acceleration in a strategically-directed revolution occurs when the leader's orders to commence operations are put into effect.

Strategies of revolution vary a great deal from one another according to the size and quality of the armed forces that revolutionary leaders must overcome and according to the ingenuity displayed by the revolutionaries. We shall discuss here only two "ideal types" of strategies – the coup d'état based on infiltration, and the militarized mass insurrection, or what is commonly known as "guerrilla warfare." Both have received a great deal of attention from twentieth-century strategists of revolution, particularly within the international communist movement, and both have resulted in outstanding instances of revolution in our time.

As a revolutionary transfer culture, a coup d'état envisions the replacement of the occupants of the existing statuses of authority with revolutionaries – men who will then utilize their newly acquired authority to initiate changes in the structure of society, sometimes including their own positions of authority, in conformity with the goal culture of the revolutionary movement. The tactic of the coup is a sudden, swift seizing, and usually killing, of a system's political elite; and its strategic success depends on one overriding condition – that the system's armed forces and the population at large welcome, or at least tolerate and therefore obey, the new occupants of the statuses of authority. As Janos has shown, this condition is never favorable to the revolutionaries unless they can already claim some position of respect or some element of legitimacy in the eyes of the population.[3] Not everyone can usurp the positions of authority and expect the army and the population to accept his explanations about why he has deposed the former rulers, even though people may be quite glad to be rid of these former rulers.

The inability of the leaders of a coup to assume automatically that their orders after the coup will be obeyed is the primary defect that a strategy of coup d'état must overcome. The main exceptions to this principle are military coups, in which the military forces can compel obedience after ousting the old elite. Even then, a *junta* can often expect that the people will call a general strike or otherwise retaliate against it. When that happens, the military must either back down or continue to govern, using totalitarian methods. In the case of the Bolsheviks' October Revolution, where Lenin and Trotsky had already gained a large measure of legitimacy in the eyes of the population, the Bolsheviks still had to form an army and consolidate their revolution in a prolonged civil war.

Modern coup d'état strategy involves either infiltrating revolutionaries into the *status quo* elite and army, or completely isolating the elite from its army and people, or both. In the communist revolutionary tradition, these techniques of coup strategy are known as the "united front," of which there are two subvarieties: the united front from above, which involves the creation of a coalition government consisting of the established elite and a communist party, and the united front from below, which involves both the legitimation of the communist party through tactical alliances with labor unions, ethnic groups, patriotic associations, and so forth, and the transformation of such groups into a front against the government. United front strategy is designed to put the revolutionaries in a position to carry out a successful coup at the highest levels of authority, maintain the continuity of authority without provoking counterrevolutions, and place members of the conspiracy in positions where they can incapacitate any challenges to the coup.

The first requirement of this strategy is the organization of the conspiratorial party itself — the unit to whom the revolutionaries will owe their primary allegiance and from whom they will take orders while serving within a united front government, labor union, army unit, or peasant cooperative. Although Lenin's ideas were foreshadowed in the eighteenth and nineteenth centuries by Babeuf, Buonarroti, and Blanqui, his formulation and implementation of the qualities of the coup party are classic: hierarchy, military command relationships, secrecy, cellular primary units, and all the rest.[4]

A second requirement of this strategy is the identification and propagandistic exploitation of the issues which will lead governments or social groups to accept coalitions with communist parties — issues such as anti-fascism, anti-imperialism, anti-militarism, etc. This is not to say that communist parties may not have genuine positions on these issues, much as other groups in a society do. However, in order for a communist party to attain a position from which it can implement its ultimate goal culture, it cannot enter a united front solely for the purpose of achieving the immediate reforms advanced by the united front. A united front is a tactical alliance that revolutionaries join in order to begin legitimatizing their movement and to position their forces for a coup d'état. A revolutionary party always has interests that go beyond the concrete issues which may allow it to form temporary alliances.

Lenin's most complete exposition and advocacy of the united front as a strategy for positioning communist parties to make coups d'état dates from 1920. In May of that year, two months before the second congress of the Communist International accepted his views as basic revolutionary strategy for the world movement, he published his *"Left-Wing" Communism, An Infantile Disorder*, subtitled, "A Popular Exposition of Marxist Strategy and Tactics." Zinoviev later compared Lenin's pamphlet to Marx's *Capital*, and Borkenau commented, " *'Left-Wing' Communism* is perhaps the most powerful thing Lenin has ever written, because it is almost free from those philosophical and economic generalizations which were not Lenin's strong point. It is a handbook of revolutionary tactics and as such can sometimes be compared, for force of argument, realism, directness, and convincing power with Machiavelli's *Il Principe*."[5]

In this handbook of revolutionary strategy, Lenin outlines the purposes of a united front: to gain for a communist party some aura of legitimacy, and to position it for making a coup d'état against its allies, when their usefulness has expired. In answer to the question, "What is the intent of the British Communist Party in entering an alliance with the Labour Party, led by Arthur Henderson, against Lloyd George?" Lenin wrote: "At present the British Communists very often find it hard to approach the masses and even to get a hearing from them. [However,] if I come out as a Communist and call upon the workers to vote for Henderson against Lloyd George, they will certainly give me a hearing. And I will be able to explain in a popular manner not only why Soviets are better than parliament and why the dictatorship of the proletariat is better than the dictatorship of Churchill (disguised by the signboard of bourgeois 'democracy'), but also that I want my vote to support Henderson *in the same way as the rope supports a hanged man* – that the impending establishment of a government of Hendersons will prove that I am right, will bring the masses over to my side, and will hasten the political death of the Hendersons and the Snowdens just as was the case with their kindred spirits in Russia and Germany."[6] Henderson, like Kerensky, was to serve as a "bridge to the new regime."

United front is the most important but not the only element in this overall strategy. In order to ensure that the army will acquiesce to a coup once it has been made, various other tasks must be performed by the Leninist party. For example, Condition Four of the Twenty-one Conditions for the admission of a national party to the Communist International, also ratified at the second Comintern congress, stresses: "The obligation to spread Communist ideas includes the special obligation to carry on systematic and energetic propaganda in the Army. Where such agitation is prevented by emergency laws, it must be carried on illegally."[7] If the army can be neutralized by such means, the coup d'état can anticipate probable success; if not, the conspirators will probably fail.

In the history of the communist movement, the Leninist coup d'état has had only a mixed record of success. In 1927, the Chinese Communist Party had successfully infiltrated a few army units and most of the labor unions, and was fully poised to make a coup against the Kuomintang, its partner in an "anti-feudal, anti-imperialist" united front, when Chiang Kai-shek carried out a coup against the communists. This development reveals the greatest weakness of the Leninist-type coup in the communist tradition: more often than not the non-communist partner in the united front is fully aware of communist intentions and can destroy the party after using it for its own purposes (e.g., as in postwar Egypt and Iraq). On the other hand, in Spain in 1936, the united front tactic worked only too well. Great Britain came to regard the Republican-Communist coalition government as a Soviet puppet, and its refusal to aid Madrid against the Axis-assisted fascist forces contributed to the eventual defeat of the Republicans. The Leninist-type coup d'état influenced the communist seizures of power in postwar eastern Europe, particularly in Czechoslovakia, but in all these changes of regime the crucial element was the presence of the Soviet Red Army. The Czech coup d'état should be considered a case of change due to exogenous forces more than to a revolution.

Contemporary Indonesia offers an example of some of the intrinsic weaknesses of Bolshevik-style tactics. In September 1965, the Indonesian Communist Party, having thoroughly infiltrated the government of President Sukarno and the Indonesian Air Force, staged a coup d'état against the regime with the ultimate intention of establishing a so-called "people's republic." The rebels accurately calculated that the army was their chief enemy, and they killed six generals in the course of implementing the coup itself. However, they did not kill Sukarno, no doubt intending to use him temporarily to legitimatize their actions, and they allowed General Haris Nasution, the Defense Minister, to escape from their net. The result was predictable: the army under Nasution reacted with ruthless measures against the party, and the people were rallied against the so-called "traitors." Thus, although the Indonesian system was definitely disequilibrated and the revolutionaries had carefully prepared their strategy, the coup failed as a result of numerous miscalculations and chance events.

The coup d'état is always an extremely risky venture, even when calculated in the most careful and realistic manner. Numerous chance factors can intervene — for example, mistaken identities, changes of schedule, unforeseen treacheries, and so forth. Its most serious defect, as Trotsky has pointed out, is that a coup can succeed without the army, but it cannot succeed against it.[8] These considerations have caused contemporary revolutionaries to shift their attention to an entirely different strategy of revolution — namely, to a direct assault on the *status quo* elite's armed forces via guerrilla warfare. Not all guerrilla revolutions have been successful (those in postwar Greece, the Philippines, and Malaya were defeated), but the record of guerrillas has been sufficiently impressive (viz., China, Algeria, Vietnam, and Yugoslavia) to make it the most widely used, and studied, strategy of revolution in the world today.

Revolutionary guerrilla warfare is an attempt to prove wrong Trotsky's principle that a revolution cannot be made *against* an entrenched elite's armed forces. It is a strategy designed to answer the question: "How does a rebel party make a revolution against a regime protected by a professional army?" The answer is complex, and acting on it is difficult. The revolutionary party must begin by turning the strengths of the elite's army into weaknesses; it must then create an army of its own; and finally it must commit its members to a long struggle. This strategy requires a greater singleness of purpose on the part of the revolutionaries than any other historical program of internal political violence.[9]

Guerrilla warfare is a form of warfare in the technical sense in which all war involves the use of armed men to annihilate the men and arms of an enemy. The initiation of a revolutionary guerrilla war thus requires that an armed band of men take to the field and launch attacks against a regime's forces. Because the military situation is by definition one in which the defending forces are far superior in strength and numbers, the rebel army's tactics are dictated by this fact. Mao Tse-tung laid down the essence of these tactics in 1929: "The enemy advances, we retreat; the enemy camps, we harass; the enemy tires, we attack; the enemy retreats, we pursue."[10] Guerrilla tactics are always employed by an objectively weaker military force against an objectively stronger military force. The guerrilla compensates for his deficiencies in training, equipment, and leadership by fighting only when, as a result of concealment or the concentration of superior numbers, victory is assured. Conversely, he flees in the face of enemy counterguerrilla campaigns, and he never offers battle on terms favorable to his foe. These are the tactical truisms of guerrilla warfare; however, the strategy of guerrilla warfare concerns not *what* the guerrilla does but *how* he is able to do it and, at the same time, begin to legitimatize the revolutionary party and prepare the population for accepting its goal culture.

The essence of guerrilla strategy is to entrap the *status quo* forces in the swamp of an overwhelmingly hostile population, and to organize this population to serve a coherent, long-range program of military conquest in which the defending force's strengths are turned into weaknesses. As Peter Paret has written: "The conquest of the population is . . . the indispensable opening of insurrectional war. Once this has been achieved, once the population has been schooled and organized for the revolutionary purpose, it becomes possible to go on to a second stage — open warfare — under conditions that are unfavorable to the enemy, even though his military forces may be larger and, according to traditional standards, better trained and equipped than those of the insurgents." [11] On this same point, Mao Tse-tung has concluded, "Because guerrilla warfare basically derives from the masses and is supported by them, it can neither exist nor flourish if it separates itself from their sympathies and cooperation." [12]

How does a revolutionary party gain the "sympathies and cooperation" of the broad mass of the people? What it needs is a general ideological appeal that will bring the revolutionary party the support of the people at the same time that it disguises any elements of the party's ultimate aspirations that might conflict with the demands of the mass movement. Promises of land redistribution to poor peasants have been used with partial success in the Asian revolutionary wars, but by far the most common appeal, and the most successful, is to the defense of the fatherland against alleged domestic traitors or foreign invaders. In order to make this appeal, the rebels may have to wait in preparation for a foreign intrusion, or else they must attempt to provoke foreign intervention so that they can arouse anti-foreign, nationalistic emotions.

Guerrillas have been known to undertake small-scale terrorism, combined with an international propaganda barrage, in order to frighten and possibly trick a foreign state into taking military action in the target system. They have also used guerrilla terror raids to intimidate a population into believing that the elite is unable to protect people from banditry, thereby causing the people in certain restricted areas temporarily to transfer their support to the guerrillas for their own safety. However, the rebels' use of terrorism to coerce support indicates that the population is basically opposed to revolutionary change, and movements based predominantly on terrorism should be analyzed as cases of subversion or crime rather than as revolutions. If a system is basically functional — and that includes being free from foreign domination or interference — efforts at artificial mobilization will fall on barren soil and be rejected. True revolutionary conditions cannot be "imported" into a social system.

Assuming that the rebel party is able to mobilize support from the people, it must then organize them for the long haul. Organization is the complement to mobilization in the strategy of guerrilla revolution. The party's "political workers" will organize the aroused populace into groups such as workers' unions, soviets, peasants' cooperatives, militia, and ascriptive associations of women, youths, and ethnic minorities. These groups will provide military support for the full-time guerrillas and give the masses a sense of participation in the revolutionary effort, thereby initiating the habits of loyalty and obedience to the legitimate authority of the rebel leaders. The final stage of organization is the establishment of revolutionary territorial bases. The government of these bases will not yet be of the form prescribed in the revolutionaries' goal culture; instead, it will be one designed to promote maximum unity and participation in the movement by all groups. As these bases are expanded and consolidated, they become a regular guerrilla "infra-structure," or an "alternative government," supplying the rebel forces with food, sanctuary, training centers, and sources of manpower. Such enclaves also weaken the *status quo* regime by removing land and population from its control.

Simultaneously with mobilization and organization, the revolutionary party begins to recruit an army. It goes without saying that this army is at first poorly trained and inadequately equipped.

However, one of its strongest characteristics is intense political fervor — an *esprit* that translates into practice as extraordinary discipline and friendly relations with the local population. Unusual standards of discipline are inculcated through rigorous indoctrination, reinforced by the irreversibility of a soldier's commitment in joining the revolutionary movement. Every guerrilla strategist, from T. E. Lawrence to Ché Guevara, has insisted on the need for intensive education of rebel soldiers. In addition to indoctrination, discipline is usually maintained through "political commissars," who are attached to and who oversee each unit of a rebel army.

Some observers have mistaken the emphasis on discipline in a well-organized guerrilla army as a sign of its humanitarianism toward the civilian population. However, while the rebels may not be anti-humanitarian, being humane is not their primary objective. In order to be effective against a professional army, the rebel forces must have the active aid of a population, not just its passive acquiescence. Only when the people provide intelligence, guides, recruits, and labor can the rebels set ambushes, avoid mopping-up campaigns, and exercise their extreme mobility. While a rebel army may be able to obtain supplies at gunpoint, it cannot get this positive support from people if it behaves like a bunch of bandits.

Intimate, friendly relations with the civilian population allow the guerrillas to obtain near-perfect intelligence concerning the enemy's strength and movements. From a military point of view, the people become a vast intelligence collecting net. This, in turn, makes possible the guerrillas' extreme mobility and freedom from logistic anchors, which enable them to set ambushes and to concentrate superior numbers at the moment of attack. The Chinese Communists regard the principle of concentration, with its attendant requisites of superior mobility and intelligence, as the key to insurrectionary warfare. A 1964 Chinese Communist theoretical publication asserts: "Starting from the basic premise of a people's war and a people's army, Mao laid down the policies and principles for building a people's army, solved a series of strategic and tactical problems concerning the way in which a people's army can defeat an enemy stronger than itself, and guided the Chinese people's armed revolutionary struggle from victory to victory. The kernel of Comrade Mao Tse-tung's thinking on the strategy and tactics of a people's war is to concentrate a superior force to destroy the enemy's forces one by one."[13] Mao himself put it more succinctly in 1937: "Our *strategy* is to pit one against ten, and our *tactics* are to pit ten against one. This is one of our fundamental principles for gaining mastery over the enemy."[14]

Guerrilla warfare is the beginning of the end of revolution, but it is not the end. Guerrilla fighting has one specific purpose: to weaken the enemy by means of a protracted war of attrition. The guerrilla phase of the revolution serves to redress the original imbalance in the respective strengths of the defending and rebel armies. The certain sign that the revolution is nearing its end is the abandonment of guerrilla tactics by the rebels in favor of massed infantry and artillery. In China, the set battle for Kaifeng (which fell on June 19, 1948) was the opening of the People's Liberation Army's final campaign to destroy the Kuomintang. Similarly, the battle for Dien Bien Phu (which fell to the Viet Minh on May 7, 1954) marked the end of the guerrilla phase and the beginning of traditional military operations against the French in Indo-China. In the latter case, there were no defenders left who wanted to fight, and the battle of Dien Bien Phu also ended the war.

Guerrilla warfare, as a strategy of revolution, is extremely difficult to defeat once it has gone so far that the defending regime must take it seriously. By the time guerrilla activities appear threatening, counterrevolutionary measures are likely to produce warfare of such savagery that the contested social system will disintegrate instead of being "won" by either the rebel or the conservative side. By far the most effective defenses against guerrilla revolution are: first, preventative and processual social change, which makes the population immune to mobilizing appeals; and second, efficient police protection against terrorists. True guerrilla revolutions are the marks of the most hopelessly intransigent opposition to change; they ought never to occur. Any form of revolution testifies to the failure of politics, but guerrilla revolutions signify the perversion of politics, the need to resort to warfare in order to oust a social group blocking change.

The two strategies of revolution discussed in this chapter illustrate a variety of tactical problems that revolutionaries encounter as well as their common, overriding strategic problem: the need to

legitimatize their resort to violence. Too often rebels have believed that the seizure of power was merely a technical problem
— that they had only to seize the "levers" of government in order
to achieve their objectives. Nothing could be further from the
truth. The resort to violence must be in response to real needs of
politically organized peoples if it is to be accepted by them as
humane, logical, and tolerable behavior. If they do not accept
revolutionary violence as such, although they may be cowed by
the force used against them, the resulting regime will be organized
more like a concentration camp than a social system. We can expect that the tactics of future revolutions will vary significantly
from case to case, but it is unlikely that the primary need to legitimatize revolutionary behavior will change.

9

The future
of revolution

ONE OF the lessons to be derived from a social systems analysis of revolutions is that they never occur as a result of forces beyond human control. Creative political action is the specific antidote to revolutionary conditions, and the occurrence of a revolution is in a sense nothing more than testimony that this antidote was not recognized or not used. In order to discover and make use of political alternatives to revolution, however, the statesman must be forewarned about situations in which revolutions may develop.

Social science can contribute to the avoidance of revolution by identifying in advance probable future instances of dissynchronization between value structures and patterns of environmental adaptation — that is, conditions requiring either politically-sanctioned change or revolutionary change. This does not mean that the social analyst can predict the occurrence of a revolution itself. As W. G. Runciman has pointed out, "The reason that social science is not analogous to meteorology is . . . that any prediction made by a social scientist is about people who can by their conscious action upset the prediction made. The proper function of social science . . . is not prediction but diagnosis."[1] In the case of diagnoses of societal disequilibria that might lead to revolution, the social scientist can only hope that his worst fears will not be realized and that political actors will bring about processual change instead of revolution. Whether or not politicians choose to act on social scientific diagnoses, however, a diagnosis is the first step toward identifying and adopting any social remedy.

Potentially revolutionary conditions in the future can be illustrated by considering the effects of two sources of change — automation and nuclear proliferation. In the highly industrialized societies of today it is widely forecast that the processes of automation, or "cybernation," will bring about a drastic change in the division of labor within a few decades. For example, Alice Mary Hilton, an associate editor of the journal *Electro-Technology*, writes: "The cybercultural revolution is of far greater magnitude than the revolution that extended the labor of man's muscle power with the machine. . . . The important difference between the mechanization that followed the first industrial revolution and automation is as fundamental as the difference in the human powers that are being replaced by machines. Automation is based on machines that are replacing the power provided by man's brains. . . . There is no doubt that the changes that are being brought about by the cybercultural revolution will be of such staggering proportions as to make the changes brought about by the first industrial revolution seem minute in comparison."[2]

The consequences of some of these "staggering" changes are not too hard to imagine. As Rex D. Hopper has observed, "The tremendous upsurge in productivity made possible by cybernation will be accompanied by a strikingly great decline in the number of people needed to keep the productive machinery going full-blast. Add to this the fact that population growth will be feeding additional millions into the job market and the magnitude of the problem of providing employment should be obvious to all but the most obstinate defender of the status quo."[3] If the values of a system in which automated technology is being introduced remain unchanged and if the applications of cybernetics remain uncontrolled, social dissynchronization of major proportions is inevitable. Moreover, it seems unlikely that homeostatic processes presently in existence will be able to resynchronize the system through evolutionary change.

Unemployment, reduced consumer purchasing power, and over-production are only the most apparent problems. Those values of Western societies which stress self-realization through meaningful and honest labor will be totally undermined, and the current prestige stratification systems cannot be maintained if the values of achievement in business, bureaucracy, or profession come to be regarded as hollow distortions of environmental realities. In these circumstances, change of some sort is easily diagnosed. Whether the change will be of a revolutionary or processual variety is much harder to foresee.

It is possible, for example, to imagine a social alternative to neo-Luddite rebellions involving the destruction of automated machines. In past centuries very large numbers of nonworking people, such as those that automation will produce, have been maintained in Europe and Asia through the institution of monasticism, either of the Christian or Buddhist varieties. It does not seem too far-fetched to imagine that there will be envalued institutions in the future which can be synchronized with an automated environment and which are likely to be the functional equivalents of monasteries. The vast expansion of universities and university applicants in the societies introducing cybernation appears to be a precursor of this trend. Institutions where large numbers of people are supported in nonadaptive activities, such as contemplation, self-cultivation, the arts, and athletics, should be anticipated in the equilibrated societies of the future.

Can even such institutions, and the values which rationalize them, be fabricated without revolution? On the one hand, it would seem that the prevailing ethics of work and achievement could only be replaced by the frontal assault of a revolutionary ideology. These ethics are simply too deeply entrenched to be easily swept away. On the other hand, if policies can be articulated for the control of cybernetic technology and for the distribution of cybernetically-manufactured products on some basis other than wages, it does not seem impossible that a system could envalue contemplation and self-cultivation over the sale of one's labor in a market. The greatest danger is that dissynchronization will become too far advanced before it is taken seriously in policy-making circles. Already the introduction of automated equipment through the method of not replacing retired labor is disguising the problem, and high rates of "structural unemployment" and artificial employment in the armed forces typify the most advanced technological societies. Whether destructive change through revolution or peaceful change through political processes will take place in order to alleviate these problems depends largely on the *political* creativity of the peoples who invented and found a use for the digital computer.

A different example of potentially revolutionary change in the future concerns the growing incapacity of the nation-state to serve as the largest self-sufficient form of social system. The progressive enlargement of the boundaries of nationally-circumscribed divisions of labor (for example, the European Common Market) is tending to dissynchronize these divisions of labor with the values that are inherent in the national-state form of regime. This is an extremely complex problem and one that has received a great deal more attention from scholars and statesmen than the unintended consequences of cybernation. We cannot review here the entire literature on supranational organization; we propose, instead, to speculate on certain selected aspects of international relations that relate directly to social systems theory and to the future of revolution.[4]

Despite numerous efforts over the past century to bring about some form of world government, either through purposive organization along political lines or through the indirect linking of national representatives in task-oriented associations (postal unions, health organizations, bodies for establishing common standards, and so forth), the national state has remained the largest form of self-contained social system. International trade and commerce have often flourished in this atmosphere, but they have never breached the principle of the nation as a self-contained whole – a fact revealed by the "economic nationalism" that rears its head, often at the cost of a good deal of domestic poverty, whenever the cherished ideals of national separateness and uniqueness appear to be threatened (for example, in Communist China after its rupture of economic ties with the Soviet Union).

Nationalism, it is endlessly and accurately repeated, remains the fundamental organizational principle of the peoples of the world, and no set of alternative values — least of all that of "proletarian internationalism" — has even begun to challenge it. In this context, nationalism should be understood as a set of political values that define and justify particular limits on a division of labor. In the past these values have in some regions "artificially" limited the technically feasible ranges within which production could have been specialized to mutual advantage, but this restriction of economic life to less than optimum levels did not inhibit the ability of a nation-state to perpetuate itself and to meet its functional requisites as a self-sufficient social system. As we have already observed, structures of values are just as capable of delimiting and defining an environment's potentialities, *within limits*, as a pattern of environmental adaptation can and does dictate the contents of values.

Have supranationalistic expansions of the limits of the division of labor at last begun to breach the capacity of nationalistic values to synchronize with them? Many scholars of so-called "regional integration," the most advanced example of which is the European Economic Community, believe that certain post-World War II forms of international economic cooperation are irreversible, and they differentiate these new forms qualitatively from older patterns of international trade, which were reversible and which did not damage the integrity of the nation-state. The degree of economic integration in the European Common Market, for example, may constitute an enlarging of the division of labor to such an extent that nationalistic structures of values cannot synchronize with it. In this case, the values of the national state would have to give way; and such a development in Europe has been repeatedly predicted, as well as hoped for, during the past two decades. However, the evidence from European experience remains inconclusive. So far, the ability of European statesmen to denounce and withdraw from any enlarged division of labor in the defense of national values has not been critically attenuated.

Nevertheless, there are other forces of change impinging on the environments of social systems that appear likely to require a future recasting of national divisions of labor and a commensurate shift in values. These forces are chiefly developments in military technology, but they also include unchecked population growth, limited national resources in water and nourishment, and extremely rapid yet socially unsupervised rates of scientific and technological innovation. One of the functional tasks of a social system is integration, which includes the peaceful resolution of conflicts of material and political interest and the control of those persons who resort to violence for whatever reason. Another functional requisite is adaptation to the environment, which includes the defense of the system from the depredations of other systems encountered in its sociopolitical environment. It seems apparent that the emerging global environment must generate needs for a type of integration and adaptation that cannot be fulfilled by social structures having nationalist values. No single nation can prevent nuclear proliferation, for example; and given an international environment in which the ownership of nuclear weapons is ubiquitous or very widespread, it is doubtful whether any single nation can permanently avoid nuclear war through deterrence. The traditionally Hobbesian quality of international relations was tolerable in the past only because the nation-state did offer a safe, self-sufficient retreat from an international state of nature; wars were an occasional occurrence, and the concepts of victory and defeat still remained credible. Today, no national state can guarantee the safety of its citizens solely on the basis of its own resources and willpower.

As the environment which was conducive to a national type of social organization changes, it seems unlikely that nationalistic values can continue to persist, despite their record of past tenacity. Supranational institutions, or their functional equivalents, would appear to be the only concrete interpretations of values that can synchronize with the rapidly emerging, new global environment. Regional organizations may proliferate and be strengthened in response to the needs of economic adaptation, but if the demands for safety and the avoidance of nuclear war are to be met, there must be, at the very least, a much closer union among the technologically advanced systems.

How might these changes from discrete national communities to transnational communities come about? Positive policies, achieved through statesmanship and negotiation — policies which reflect a knowledge of environmental realities and whose wisdom is accepted by national populations — may alter the values of national state systems through peaceful processes. But these changes may equally well be achieved through revolution. If nationalist leaders remain intransigently opposed to changes in the national form of sovereignty and if their populations become informed of the dangers of this course of action, such leaders may provoke revolutions against themselves. The fact that no such anti-nationalist revolts have as yet materialized reflects the persisting strength of the nationalist ethos, but the conditions in which this ethos may continue to dominate events are altering rapidly against it.

It is possible that the world of the future will contain only one social system (with numerous subsystems), and such a possibility raises again the meaning of the distinction between war and revolution. Insofar as we distinguish between the two on the basis of whether violence is intersystemic or intrasystemic, it is clear that war would disappear in the global social system. We would predict, then, that as the condition of a single social system is approached, violent attempts to bring about social change will increasingly take the forms of rebellion or revolution — that is, of civil war rather than intersystemic war. Although a single social system is still no more than an ideal at the present time, some relations of conflict between nations have already begun to resemble intrasystemic violence. For example, a near consensus on the need to avoid nuclear war appears to have developed, and possible future wars between an alliance of the technically advanced systems against atomically nonconforming powers, such as China or France, might best be studied as cases of the suppression of rebellion — always assuming there is someone left to do the studying.

In this chapter we have speculated broadly about some of the most general sources of change that are likely to make future demands on men's political ingenuity. There are, of course, numerous other sources of change, and it would be folly to suppose that the political vision of human beings is sufficient to bring about processual change in all, or even the most important, of these cases. According to Eckstein's count, between 1946 and 1959 alone, there occurred some 1,200 unequivocal instances of guerrilla war, organized terrorism, mutiny, coup d'état, and so forth.[5] Therefore, barring some unforeseen improvement in men's political judgment, the future of revolution seems assured.

N otes

CHAPTER I. REVOLUTION: THE IMPLICATIONS
OF A POLITICAL CONCEPT

1. Arthur Bauer, *Essai sur les Révolutions* (Paris: Giard & Brière, 1908), Bibliothèque Sociologique Internationale, XXXVI, p. 11.
2. Hannah Arendt, *On Revolution* (New York: Viking Press, 1963), p. 9.
3. Arthur Hatto, " 'Revolution': An Enquiry into the Usefulness of an Historical Term," *Mind*, LVIII, No. 232 (October 1949), 495–517.
4. Aristotle, *Politics*, Benjamin Jowett trans., reprinted in William Ebenstein, *Great Political Thinkers* (New York: Rinehart & Co., 1951), p. 106.
5. Gaetano Salvemini quoted by Kenneth E. Bock, "Evolution and Historical Process," *American Anthropologist*, LIV (1952), 494.
6. Crane Brinton, *Anatomy of Revolution* (Englewood Cliffs, N.J.: Prentice-Hall, 1938).
7. Harry Eckstein, ed., *Internal War, Problems and Approaches* (New York: The Free Press of Glencoe, 1964), p. 23. For a survey of analytical approaches to the study of revolution, see Lawrence Stone, "Theories of Revolution," *World Politics*, XVIII, No. 2 (January 1966), 159–76.

8. Alfred H. Stanton and Stewart E. Percy, eds., *Personality and Political Crisis* (Glencoe, Ill.: Free Press, 1951), p. 10. Another objection to comparative analyses of revolutions in the absence of a thorough conceptualization of revolution is that "In human affairs a causal generalization derived entirely from a set of analogous events is undependable, for the simple reason that human beings sometimes profit from experience." Louis Gottschalk, "Causes of Revolution," *The American Journal of Sociology*, L, No. 1 (July 1944), 3.

9. Max Weber, *The Theory of Social and Economic Organization*, A. M. Henderson and Talcott Parsons, trans. (New York: The Free Press of Glencoe, paperbound ed., 1964), p. 88.

10. Thomas Hobbes, *Leviathan* (1651), Part I, Chapter xiii.

11. Norton Long, "The Political Act as an Act of Will," *The American Journal of Sociology*, LXIX (July 1963), 1.

12. For example, Stanislaw Andrzejewski, *Military Organization and Society* (London: Routledge & Kegan Paul, 1954), p. 22.

13. Lewis Coser, *The Functions of Social Conflict* (Glencoe, Ill.: Free Press, 1956), p. 21.

14. Talcott Parsons and Edward A. Shils, *Toward A General Theory of Action: Theoretical Foundations for the Social Sciences* (New York: Harper Torchbooks, paperbound ed., 1962), p. 231. Emphasis in the original.

15. Reinhard Bendix, *Nation-Building and Citizenship* (New York: John Wiley & Sons, 1964), p. 45.

16. Ortega y Gasset, *The Revolt of the Masses* (New York: W. W. Norton & Co., 1932), p. 82.

17. Eckstein, *op. cit.*, p. 13.

18. Arendt, *op. cit.*, p. 2.

19. See Max Gluckman, *Order and Rebellion in Tribal Africa* (New York: The Free Press of Glencoe, 1963).

CHAPTER 2.   THE SOCIAL SYSTEM: COERCION
AND VALUES

1. Dorothy Emmet, *Function, Purpose and Powers* (London: Macmillan, 1958), p. 23.

2. *Ibid.*, p. 16.

3. Thomas Hobbes, *Leviathan* (1651), Part I, Chapter xiii.

4. Ralf Dahrendorf, *Class and Class Conflict in Industrial Society* (Stanford, Calif.: Stanford University Press, 1959), p. 64.

5. Max Weber, *From Max Weber: Essays in Sociology*, H. H. Gerth

and C. Wright Mills, trans. (New York: Oxford Galaxy Book, 1958), p. 78. Emphasis in the original.

6. Dahrendorf, *op. cit.*, pp. 21, 30–31, 137.

7. *Ibid.*, p. 165.

8. Translated and quoted by Dahrendorf, *ibid.*, p. 14.

9. Talcott Parsons, "Some Reflections on the Place of Force in Social Process," in Harry Eckstein, ed., *Internal War, Problems and Approaches* (New York: The Free Press of Glencoe, 1964), p. 34.

10. Talcott Parsons, *The Social System* (New York: The Free Press of Glencoe, paperbound ed., 1964), p. 42.

11. Thomas Kuhn, *The Structure of Scientific Revolutions* (Chicago: University of Chicago Press, 1962), p. x.

12. Talcott Parsons, "Authority, Legitimation, and Political Action," in C. J. Friedrich, ed., *Authority* (Cambridge, Mass.: Harvard University Press, 1958), p. 199.

13. Philip E. Jacob, "The Influence of Values in Political Integration," in P. E. Jacob, *et al.*, eds., *The Integration of Political Communities* (Philadelphia: J. B. Lippincott Co., paperbound ed., 1964), p. 220.

14. D. F. Aberle, A. K. Cohen, A. K. Davis, M. J. Levy, F. X. Sutton, "The Functional Prerequisites of a Society," *Ethics*, LX (January 1950), 100–11.

15. Anthony F. C. Wallace, *Culture and Personality* (New York: Random House Studies in Anthropology, paperbound ed., 1961), pp. 26–27.

16. *Ibid.*, p. 40.

17. *Ibid.*, p. 41.

18. See James C. Davies, *Human Nature in Politics* (New York: John Wiley & Sons, 1963), p. 9. For an extended discussion of needs and a different conception of them, see H. G. Barnett, *Innovation: The Basis of Cultural Change* (New York: McGraw-Hill, paperbound ed., 1953), Part 2, pp. 97–180.

19. Thomas Carlyle, *On Heroes and Hero-Worship* (1840) (New York: Doubleday Dolphin Books, paperbound ed., n.d.), pp. 13–14. Compare K. E. Boulding, "The Place of the Image in the Dynamics of Society," in G. K. Zollschan and W. Hirsch, eds., *Explorations in Social Change* (Boston: Houghton Mifflin, 1964), pp. 5–16, particularly pp. 10–13.

20. On the question of whether these inescapable discriminations are, indeed, inescapable, see: Kingsley Davis and Wilbert E. Moore, "Some Principles of Stratification," *American Sociological Review*, X (April 1945), 242–49; Melvin Tumin, "Some Principles of

Stratification: A Critical Analysis," *ibid.*, XVIII (August 1953), 387–97 (with replies by Davis and Moore); and Dennis H. Wrong, "The Functional Theory of Stratification: Some Neglected Considerations," *ibid.*, XXIV (December 1959), 772–82.

21. Max Weber, *The Theory of Social and Economic Organization*, A. M. Henderson and Talcott Parsons, trans. (New York: The Free Press of Glencoe, paperbound ed., 1964), p. 152.

22. Dahrendorf, *op. cit.*, p. 166.

23. Parsons, in *Internal War*, p. 42.

24. *Ibid.*, p. 45.

25. *Ibid.*, p. 46.

26. *Ibid.*, p. 47.

27. *Ibid.*, pp. 34–39.

28. Hannah Arendt, *On Revolution* (New York: Viking Press, 1963), p. 153.

29. *Ibid.*, p. 112.

30. See Parsons, *The Social System*, pp. 252, 267 *et seq.*

31. Quoted by George Woodcock, *Anarchism* (Cleveland: World Meridian Books, 1962), p. 276.

32. Cf. Norton Long, "The Political Act as an Act of Will," *The American Journal of Sociology*, LXIX (July 1963), 1–2.

33. See James Joll, *The Anarchists* (London: Eyre & Spottiswoode, 1964), p. 55.

34. Quoted by Joll, *ibid.*, pp. 75–76.

35. Dahrendorf, *op. cit.*, p. 135.

36. See Vilhelm Aubert, "Competition and Dissensus: Two Types of Conflict and of Conflict Resolution," *The Journal of Conflict Resolution*, VII, No. 1 (1963), 26–42.

37. Dahrendorf, *op. cit.*, p. 178.

38. David Lockwood, "Some Remarks on 'The Social System,'" *The British Journal of Sociology*, VII, No. 2 (June 1956), 140. Also see Lockwood, "Social Integration and System Integration," in Zollschan and Hirsch, eds., *op. cit.*, pp. 244–57.

CHAPTER 3. THE SOCIAL SYSTEM: STRUCTURE AND FUNCTION

1. See Alvin W. Gouldner, "Reciprocity and Autonomy in Functional Theory," in Llewellyn Gross, ed., *Symposium on Sociological Theory* (New York: Harper & Row, 1959), p. 242.

2. D. F. Aberle, *et al.*, "The Functional Prerequisites of a Society," *Ethics*, LX (January 1950), 101.

3. Alfred H. Stanton and Stewart E. Percy, eds., *Personality and Political Crisis* (Glencoe, Ill.: Free Press, 1951), p. 81.

4. For a discussion of variations in role performances of Supreme Court justices, see, for example, Anthony Lewis, *Gideon's Trumpet* (New York: Random House, 1964).

5. Wilbert E. Moore, *Social Change* (Englewood Cliffs, N.J.: Prentice-Hall, 1963), p. 13.

6. Aberle, *et al.*, *op. cit.*, p. 105.

7. Dorothy Emmet, *Function, Purpose and Powers* (London: Macmillan, 1958), p. 26.

8. Ralf Dahrendorf, *Class and Class Conflict in Industrial Society* (Stanford, Calif.: Stanford University Press, 1959), p. 120.

9. Emmet, *op. cit.*, p. 113.

10. *Ibid.*, p. 57. See also Charles Taylor, *The Explanation of Behaviour* (London: Routledge & Kegan Paul, 1964).

11. *Ibid.*, pp. 84, 96.

12. For a warning concerning the dangers of "normative functionalism," see Lewis Coser, "Social Conflict and the Theory of Social Change," *The British Journal of Sociology*, VII (September 1957), 206–207, n. 22; and David Lockwood, in G. K. Zollschan and W. Hirsch, eds., *Explorations in Social Change* (Boston: Houghton Mifflin, 1964), p. 245.

13. Talcott Parsons, *Essays in Sociological Theory: Pure and Applied* (Glencoe, Ill.: Free Press, 1949), p. 21. Quoted by Gouldner, *op. cit.*, p. 243.

14. Gouldner, *op. cit.*, p. 241.

15. Aberle, *et al.*, *op. cit.*, *passim*. The Aberle prerequisites have been rephrased as positive actions rather than left as conditions.

16. For a summary and application of the Parsonian "functional imperatives," see Karl Deutsch, "Integration and the Social System: Implications of Functional Analysis," in P. E. Jacob, *et al.*, eds., *The Integration of Political Communities* (Philadelphia: J. B. Lippincott Co., paperbound ed., 1964), pp. 179–208.

17. Carl Hempel, in L. Gross, ed., *op. cit.*, p. 294.

18. Emmet, *op. cit.*, p. 74.

19. *Ibid.*, p. 62.

20. Anthony F. C. Wallace, "Revitalization Movements," *American Anthropologist*, LVIII (April 1956), 265.

21. Dahrendorf, *op. cit.*, p. 225.

22. *Ibid.*, p. 121.

CHAPTER 4. THE DISEQUILIBRATED SOCIAL SYSTEM

1. Eric Hoffer, *The Ordeal of Change* (New York: Harper Colophon Books, paperbound ed., 1964), pp. 4–5.
2. T. H. Wintringham, *Mutiny* (London: Stanley Nott, 1936), p. 10.
3. Louis Gottschalk, "Causes of Revolution," *The American Journal of Sociology*, L, No. 1 (July 1944), 5.
4. Anthony F. C. Wallace, *Culture and Personality* (New York: Random House Studies in Anthropology, paperbound ed., 1961), p. 144.
5. Hoffer, *op. cit.*, p. 84.
6. Alexander Gerschenkron, "Reflections on Economic Aspects of Revolutions," in Harry Eckstein, ed., *Internal War, Problems and Approaches* (New York: The Free Press of Glencoe, 1964), p. 185.
7. Alexis de Tocqueville, *The Old Régime and the French Revolution*, Stuart Gilbert, trans. (New York: Doubleday Anchor Books, paperbound ed., 1955), p. 176.
8. James C. Davies, "Toward a Theory of Revolution," *American Sociological Review*, XXVII, No. 1 (February 1962), 6, 8; and *Human Nature in Politics* (New York: John Wiley & Sons, 1963), p. 350.
9. Alfred Meusel, "Revolution and Counter-Revolution," *Encyclopedia of the Social Sciences*, XIII (1934), 367.
10. H. G. Barnett, *Innovation: The Basis of Cultural Change* (New York: McGraw-Hill, paperbound ed., 1953), p. 80.
11. Wilbert E. Moore, *Social Change* (Englewood Cliffs, N.J.: Prentice-Hall, 1963), p. 18.
12. Quoted by Arthur Bauer, *Essai sur les Révolutions* (Paris: Giard & Brière, 1908), Bibliothèque Sociologique Internationale, XXXVI, p. 41.
13. Everett Hagen, *On the Theory of Social Change* (Homewood, Ill.: The Dorsey Press, 1962), p. 6.
14. See Wallace, *op. cit.*, p. 125; and Everett M. Rogers, *Diffusion of Innovations* (New York: The Free Press of Glencoe, 1962), *passim*.
15. Barnett, *op. cit.*, pp. 181 *et seq.*
16. *Ibid.*, p. 56.
17. See George M. Foster, *Traditional Cultures: And The Impact of Technological Change* (New York: Harper & Row, 1962), pp. 112–15; and Everett C. Hughes, "Social Change and Status Pro-

test: An Essay on the Marginal Man," *Phylon*, X (first quarter, 1949), 58–65.

18. On modernizing oligarchs, see Edward Shils, *Political Development in the New States* (The Hague: Mouton, 1962), pp. 67ff.

19. For a case study of a high-status innovator, see L. Pospisil, "Social Change and Primitive Law: Consequences of a Papuan Legal Case," *American Anthropologist*, LX (1958), 832–37; and E. R. Leach, "Social Change and Primitive Law [Rejoinder]," *ibid.*, LXI (1959), 1096–97.

20. Karl Deutsch, "Social Mobilization and Political Development," *American Political Science Review*, LV, No. 3 (September 1961), 493–514.

21. Hoffer, *op. cit.*, pp. 120–21.

22. Basic bibliography is included in A. James Gregor, "Black Nationalism: A Preliminary Analysis of Negro Radicalism," *Science and Society*, XXVII, No. 4 (Fall 1963), 415–32.

23. George S. Pettee, *The Process of Revolution* (New York: Harper Bros., 1938), p. 66.

24. Anthony F. C. Wallace, "Revitalization Movements," *American Anthropologist*, LVIII (April 1956), 266.

25. Wallace, *Culture and Personality*, p. 20.

26. Emile Durkheim, *The Rules of Sociological Method* (Glencoe, Ill.: Free Press, 1938, 1950), pp. lvi–lvii, n. 7.

27. Talcott Parsons, "Personality and Social Structure," in Alfred H. Stanton and Stewart E. Percy, eds., *Personality and Political Crisis* (Glencoe, Ill.: Free Press, 1951), p. 74. Emphasis added.

28. Donald R. Cressey, "The Respectable Criminal," *Trans-Action* (March-April 1965), pp. 12–15.

29. Parsons, in *Personality and Political Crisis*, pp. 72–74.

30. Herbert Phillips, "Personality and Social Structure in a Siamese Community," *Human Organization*, XXII, No. 2 (1963), 105.

31. See, for example, Eric Hoffer, *The True Believer* (New York: Mentor Books, paperbound ed., 1958).

32. Harold D. Lasswell, *Psychopathology and Politics* (New York: Viking Compass Books, paperbound ed., 1960), pp. 180–81.

33. P. M. Yap, "The Mental Illness of Hung Hsiu-ch'üan, Leader of the Taiping Rebellion," *Far Eastern Quarterly*, XIII, No. 3 (May 1954), 287–304.

34. Wallace, *Culture and Personality*, p. 152.

35. A. Inkeles and D. J. Levinson, "National Character: The Study of Modal Personality and Sociocultural Systems," in Gardner

Lindzey, ed., *Handbook of Social Psychology* (Reading, Mass.: Addison-Wesley, 1954), p. 982.

36. Lewis Coser, *The Functions of Social Conflict* (New York: The Free Press of Glencoe, paperbound ed., 1964), p. 78.

37. Talcott Parsons, *The Social System* (New York: The Free Press of Glencoe, paperbound ed., 1964), p. 521.

38. Kurt Riezler, "On the Psychology of the Modern Revolution," *Social Research*, X, No. 3 (September 1943), 320–26.

39. Erik Erikson, *Young Man Luther* (New York: W. W. Norton Library, paperbound ed., 1962), p. 22.

40. Parsons, in *Internal War*, p. 66.

41. Clifford Geertz, "Ideology as a Cultural System," in David E. Apter, ed., *Ideology and Discontent* (New York: The Free Press of Glencoe, 1964), p. 64.

42. Wallace, *Culture and Personality*, p. 148.

43. See Rev. James J. Maguire, *The Philosophy of Modern Revolution* (Washington: The Catholic University of America Philosophical Studies, LXXIV, 1943), 76–77; and Chalmers Johnson, *Revolution and the Social System* (Stanford, Calif.: Hoover Institution Studies, No. 3, 1964), 35–39.

44. Parsons, *The Social System*, p. 530.

45. An excellent case study of the transformation of Bolshevik revolutionary ideology into the value structure of the Soviet Union is Raymond A. Bauer, *The New Man in Soviet Psychology* (Cambridge, Mass.: Harvard University Press, 1959).

46. Alexis de Tocqueville, *The Old Régime and the French Revolution*, Stuart Gilbert, trans. (New York: Doubleday Anchor Books, paperbound ed., 1955), p. 13.

47. Thomas Carlyle, *On Heroes and Hero-Worship* (1840) (New York: Doubleday Dolphin Books, paperbound ed., n.d.), pp. 121–22.

CHAPTER 5. REVOLUTION

1. Karl Popper, *The Poverty of Historicism* (New York: Harper Torchbooks, paperbound ed., 1964), p. 66.

2. Dorothy Emmet, *Function, Purpose and Powers* (London: Macmillan, 1958), pp. 105–106.

3. Niccolò Machiavelli, *The Prince and The Discourses* (New York: Modern Library, 1940), p. 81.

4. Lucian Pye, "Roots of Insurgency," in Harry Eckstein, ed., *Internal*

War, Problems and Approaches (New York: The Free Press of Glencoe, 1964), pp. 159–60.

5. Lewis Namier, *1848: The Revolution of the Intellectuals* (New York: Doubleday Anchor Books, paperbound ed., 1964), p. 3.

6. *Ibid.*, p. 26.

7. George S. Pettee, *The Process of Revolution* (New York: Harper Bros., 1938), p. 91.

8. See *The New York Times*, May 7, 8, 1965.

9. Pettee, *op. cit.*, p. 11.

10. Stanislaw Andrzejewski, *Military Organization and Society* (London: Routledge & Kegan Paul, 1954), pp. 158, 127.

11. Alexis de Tocqueville, *The Old Régime and the French Revolution*, Stuart Gilbert, trans. (New York: Doubleday Anchor Books, paperbound ed., 1955), p. 20.

12. Louis Gottschalk, "Causes of Revolution," *The American Journal of Sociology*, L, No. 1 (July 1944), 8.

13. Peter Amann, "Revolution: A Redefinition," *Political Science Quarterly*, LXXVII, No. 1 (March 1962), 39.

14. Pettee, *op. cit.*, p. 100.

15. Katharine C. Chorley, *Armies and the Art of Revolution* (London: Faber & Faber, 1943), pp. 11, 16.

16. Cecil Woodham-Smith, *The Reason Why* (New York: McGraw-Hill, 1953; Time Special ed., 1962), p. 26.

17. Chorley, *op. cit.*, p. 87.

18. United Nations, XI General Assembly, *Report of the Special Committee on the Problem of Hungary* (A/3592, 1957), pp. 24–25, s. v. pars. 159, 166.

19. F. M. Cornford, trans., *The Republic of Plato* (New York: Oxford University Press, 1945), p. 268.

20. Chorley, *op. cit.*, p. 108.

21. For the relationship between war and revolution in China and Yugoslavia, see Chalmers Johnson, *Peasant Nationalism and Communist Power* (Stanford, Calif.: Stanford University Press, 1962).

22. Chorley, *op. cit.*, p. 76.

23. Anthony F. C. Wallace, *Culture and Personality* (New York: Random House Studies in Anthropology, paperbound ed., 1961), pp. 143–44.

24. Anthony F. C. Wallace, "Revitalization Movements," *American Anthropologist*, LVIII (April 1956), 264.

25. Wallace, *Culture and Personality*, p. 144. Italics added.

26. *Ibid.*, 147.

27. *Ibid.*
28. *Ibid.*
29. *Ibid.*, p. 148.
30. Theodora Kroeber, *Ishi in Two Worlds* (Berkeley: University of California Press, 1962).
31. Wallace, *Culture and Personality*, p. 149.
32. *Ibid.*, p. 151.
33. Hannah Arendt, *On Revolution* (New York: Viking Press, 1963), p. 235.
34. Wallace, *Culture and Personality*, pp. 160–61.
35. Thomas Kuhn, *The Structure of Scientific Revolutions* (Chicago: University of Chicago Press, 1962), pp. 65, 77, 144.
36. Wallace, *Culture and Personality*, p. 161.
37. John Locke, *Two Treatises of Government*, Thomas I. Cook, ed. (New York: Hafner Publishing Co., 1947), p. 233.
38. *Ibid.*, p. 207.
39. *Ibid.*, p. 238.
40. *Ibid.*, p. 235.
41. *Ibid.*, p. 225.
42. *Ibid.*, p. 236.
43. *Ibid.*, p. 244.
44. *Ibid.*, pp. 233–34.
45. Arendt, *op. cit.*, p. 18.
46. *Ibid.*, p. 158.
47. *Ibid.*, p. 28.
48. *Ibid.*, p. 121.
49. *Ibid.*
50. *Ibid.*, p. 221.

CHAPTER 6. MEASURING DISEQUILIBRIUM

1. Arnold Feldman, "Violence and Volatility: The Likelihood of Revolution," in Harry Eckstein, ed., *Internal War, Problems and Approaches* (New York: The Free Press of Glencoe, 1964), p. 115.
2. Walt W. Rostow, *British Economy of the Nineteenth Century* (Oxford: Clarendon Press, 1948); and Ronald G. Ridker, "Discontent and Economic Growth," *Economic Development and Cultural Change*, XI, No. 1 (October 1962), 1–15.
3. For a recent research project which is beset by these shortcomings, see Charles Tilly and James Rule, *Measuring Political Upheaval* (Princeton: Center of International Studies, 1965).

4. Emile Durkheim, *Suicide*, John A. Spaulding and George Simpson, trans. (Glencoe, Ill.: Free Press, 1951), p. 208.

5. Andrew F. Henry and James F. Short, Jr., *Suicide and Homicide, Some Economic, Sociological and Psychological Aspects of Aggression* (Glencoe, Ill.: Free Press, 1954), p. 13.

6. A. L. Wood, *Crime and Aggression in Changing Ceylon: A Sociological Analysis of Homicide, Suicide, and Economic Crime* (Philadelphia: The American Philosophical Society Transactions, LI, part 8, 1961), 91.

7. Louis I. Dublin, *Suicide: A Sociological and Statistical Study* (New York: The Ronald Press, 1963), p. 209.

8. Robert Shogan and Tom Craig, *The Detroit Race Riot* (Philadelphia: Chilton Books, 1964), pp. 32–33.

CHAPTER 7. VARIETIES OF REVOLUTION

1. Hannah Arendt, *On Revolution* (New York: Viking Press, 1963), p. 33.

2. E. J. Hobsbawm, *The Age of Revolution, 1789–1848* (Cleveland: World Publishing Co., 1962), p. 160.

3. George Woodcock, *Anarchism* (Cleveland: World Meridian Books, 1962), p. 469.

4. The present use of the terms "government," "regime," and "community" follows that of David Easton, in "Political Anthropology," *Biennial Review of Anthropology 1959*, B. J. Siegal, ed. (Stanford, Calif.: Stanford University Press, 1959), pp. 228–29.

5. James Rosenau, ed., *International Aspects of Civil Strife* (Princeton: Princeton University Press, 1964), pp. 63–64.

6. Anthony F. C. Wallace, "Revitalization Movements," *American Anthropologist*, LVIII (April 1956), 275.

7. *Ibid.*, p. 276.

8. An example of research that roots revolution in the context of the disequilibrated system — a study that could well serve as a model for further work on political violence — is Charles Tilly, *The Vendée, A Sociological Analysis of the Counterrevolution of 1793* (Cambridge, Mass.: Harvard University Press, 1964).

9. Talcott Parsons and Edward A. Shils, eds., *Toward a General Theory of Action: Theoretical Foundations for the Social Sciences* (New York: Harper Torchbooks, paperbound ed., 1962), p. 76.

10. For a study of interdependence and equilibrium as variables which differentiate types of social systems, see Alvin W. Gouldner, "Reciprocity and Autonomy in Functional Theory," in Llewellyn

Gross, ed., *Symposium on Sociological Theory* (New York: Harper & Row, 1959), pp. 241–70.

11. Cf. Tilly, *The Vendée*, p. 16.

12. *Ibid.*, p. 17.

13. Arnold Feldman, "Violence and Volatility: The Likelihood of Revolution," in Harry Eckstein, ed., *Internal War, Problems and Approaches* (New York: The Free Press of Glencoe, 1964), pp. 120–21.

14. See Gabriel A. Almond and Sidney Verba, *The Civic Culture* (Princeton: Princeton University Press, 1963).

CHAPTER 8. STRATEGIES OF REVOLUTION

1. Thomas Schelling, *The Strategy of Conflict* (New York: Oxford Galaxy Books, paperbound ed., 1963), p. 3. Italics in original.

2. *Ibid.*, p. 90.

3. Andrew C. Janos, *The Seizure of Power, A Study of Force and Popular Consent* (Princeton: Center of International Studies, 1964), pp. 36–39.

4. See Chalmers Johnson, *Revolution and the Social System* (Stanford, Calif.: Hoover Institution Studies, No. 3, 1964), pp. 49–57. For a complete discussion of Leninist tactics of infiltration, see Philip Selznick, *The Organizational Weapon* (Glencoe, Ill.: Free Press, 1960).

5. Franz Borkenau, *World Communism* (Ann Arbor: University of Michigan Press, paperbound ed., 1962), p. 191.

6. V. I. Lenin, *"Left-Wing" Communism, An Infantile Disorder* (Moscow: Foreign Languages Publishing House, n.d.), p. 85. Italics added.

7. In Gunther Nollau, *International Communism and World Revolution: History and Methods* (New York: Frederick A. Praeger, 1961), p. 341.

8. Leon Trotsky, *The Russian Revolution*, abridged ed. (New York: Doubleday Anchor Books, paperbound ed., 1959), p. 318. Quoted by Janos, *op. cit.*, p. 55.

9. For more detailed studies of guerrilla warfare, see Chalmers Johnson, "Civilian Loyalties and Guerrilla Conflict," *World Politics*, XIV, No. 4 (July 1962), 646–61, also available in U.S. Air Force Academy Associates, *United States Defense Policy* (Baltimore: The Johns Hopkins Press, 1965); and *Revolution and the Social System*, pp. 57–69.

10. *Mao Tse-tung hsüan-chi* [Selected Works of Mao Tse-tung] (Peking: Jen-min ch'u-pan-she, 1964), I, 107.
11. Peter Paret, "The French Army and *La Guerre Révolutionnaire*," *Journal of the Royal United Service Institution*, CIV, No. 613 (February 1959), 59.
12. *Mao Tse-tung on Guerrilla Warfare*, S. Griffith, trans. (New York: Frederick A. Praeger, 1961), p. 44.
13. *Peking Review*, No. 15 (April 9, 1965), p. 12.
14. *Mao Tse-tung hsüan-chi*, I, 219.

CHAPTER 9.   THE FUTURE OF REVOLUTION

1. W. G. Runciman, *Social Science and Political Theory* (Cambridge: Cambridge University Press, 1963), p. 17.
2. Alice Mary Hilton, *Logic, Computing Machines, and Automation* (Washington: Spartan Books, 1963), pp. 371, 378; quoted in Rex D. Hopper, "Cybernation, Marginality, and Revolution," Special Operations Research Office, Washington, mimeo. An abridged version of Hopper's paper was published in I. L. Horowitz, ed., *The New Sociology* (New York: Oxford University Press, 1964), pp. 313–30.
3. Hopper, *op. cit.*, p. 36.
4. See Ernst B. Haas, *Beyond the Nation-State, Functionalism and International Organization* (Stanford, Calif.: Stanford University Press, 1964), parts I and III.
5. Harry Eckstein, ed., *Internal War, Problems and Approaches* (New York: The Free Press of Glencoe, 1964), p. 3.

Index